An 8-Week Transformational Bible Study
of **HABAKKUK**

embracing

joy

Our Daily Bread
Publishing™

JEAN WILUND

Embracing Joy: An 8-Week Transformational Bible Study of Habakkuk
© 2023 by Jean Wilund

Requests for permission to quote from this book should be directed to: Permissions Department, Our Daily Bread Publishing, PO Box 3566, Grand Rapids, MI 49501, or contact us by email at permissionsdept@odb.org.

Scripture quotations, unless otherwise indicated, are taken from the ESV® Bible (The Holy Bible, English Standard Version®), copyright © 2001 by Crossway, a publishing ministry of Good News Publishers. Used by permission. All rights reserved.

Scripture quotations marked HCSB are from the Holman Christian Standard Bible®. Copyright © 1999, 2000, 2002, 2003, 2009 by Holman Bible Publishers. Used by permission. Holman Christian Standard Bible®, Holman CSB®, and HCSB® are federally registered trademarks of Holman Bible Publishers.

Scripture quotations marked NIV are taken from the Holy Bible, New International Version®, NIV®. Copyright © 1973, 1978, 1984, 2011 by Biblica, Inc.™ Used by permission of Zondervan. All rights reserved worldwide. www.zondervan.com.

Scripture quotations marked NKJV are taken from the New King James Version®. Copyright © 1982 by Thomas Nelson. Used by permission. All rights reserved.

Throughout, italics have been added by the author for emphasis.

Interior design by Gayle Raymer

Library of Congress Cataloging-in-Publication Data

Names: Wilund, Jean, author.
Title: Embracing joy : a transformational Bible study of Habakkuk / Jean Wilund.
Description: Grand Rapids, MI : Our Daily Bread Publishing, [2023] | Summary: "Learn from the complicated life and world of Habakkuk"-- Provided by publisher.
Identifiers: LCCN 2022060038 | ISBN 9781640702318 (trade paperback) | ISBN 9781640702431 (epub)
Subjects: LCSH: Bible. Habakkuk--Textbooks. | Joy--Biblical teaching--Textbooks. | BISAC: RELIGION / Biblical Studies / Old Testament / Prophets | RELIGION / Christian Living / Spiritual Growth
Classification: LCC BS1635.52 .W55 2023 | DDC 224/.95--dc23/eng/20230306
LC record available at https://lccn.loc.gov/2022060038

Printed in the United States of America
23 24 25 26 27 28 29 30 / 8 7 6 5 4 3 2 1

contents

To Grace Hamrick

My patient mentor, beloved friend, and a
woman after God's own heart.
God poured out His superabundant grace and
mercy on me the day He saved me and the day
He sent you into my life. Both days
transformed me forever.
Thank you for the hours you've spent discipling
me to know and believe God and His Word—
and to love Him with my whole heart. Many
of the truths in this study, I first learned at your
side. They have never failed me.
I love you!

Why Would I Want to Study Habakkuk?

When I announced my plan to teach a Bible study on Habakkuk, a friend said, "Why would you want to study such a depressing book?"

I laughed because years ago, I would've said the same thing. I would've summarized Habakkuk as a book about God's people losing everything. Whoopee! Sign me up to study that book.

However, Habakkuk's final words remained in my mind: "Yet I will rejoice in the LORD; I will take joy in the God of my salvation" (3:18).

How could Habakkuk rejoice in such devastation? When all was gloom and despair, how did joy find a place in his heart? Either Habakkuk had gone mad, or he knew a secret—a truth—I needed to know.

I grabbed my Bible and set out to discover his secret.

I probably flipped past Habakkuk five times trying to find it buried between the equally short books of Nahum and Zephaniah. It only took me five minutes and nine seconds to read Habakkuk (yes, I timed it). It took even less time for me to become enthralled and encouraged by Habakkuk's words. (This time.) I couldn't wait to dig deeper.

This minor prophet with a major message staggered in the face of cataclysmic news, but God transformed Habakkuk's panic into praise and his confusion into confidence. Sure-footed faith led him to joy in the Lord despite the imminent destruction of his people's kingdom, cities, and for some, even their lives. Habakkuk's experience can be ours if we'll follow his example. What we discover in these three short chapters will prepare us to face the future—and smile.

No matter what happens tomorrow, Habakkuk proves we can rejoice today—and forevermore.

Let the journey begin!

Jean

How to Get the Most Out of This Study

First things first. Are you wondering how to pronounce Habakkuk? I've heard it pronounced more ways than I thought possible even by scholars. I've settled on pastor and commentator O. Palmer Robertson's pronunciation of Habakkuk—huh-BAK-uhk.[1]

THE TRANSFORMATIONAL BIBLE STUDY METHOD

Understanding Habakkuk can be challenging, but the Transformational Bible Study Method makes it easier. This three-step method moves us from simply gaining information to experiencing genuine transformation. We'll look at it closely in week one.

1. **Intent:** What was the author's intent to his original audience?
2. **Truth:** What truths does God's Word reveal about the character, nature, and ways of God, and that of anyone or anything other than God?
3. **Transformation:** If I truly believe and act on what God has revealed in this passage, how will the motivations and attitudes of my heart transform and my actions be different tomorrow?

STUDYING WITH A GROUP

I've included group study questions at the end of each week. I recommend the participants work through each week's lesson at home, prior to meeting with your group. For the first week, before you work through the lesson, watch the free introduction video on the Habakkuk resource page of my website (JeanWilund.com). Then come together as a group to review and discuss the questions.

Consider planning a celebration meal at the end of your study. Encourage the group members to share what God has done in their hearts and minds over the course of the study, and close the time with prayer.

ADDITIONAL RESOURCES

For helpful resources, visit the Habakkuk resource page on my website (JeanWilund.com).

seeing

rightly

As we begin this transformational study, let's take a brief assessment.

What one word describes the state of your heart right now?

_____

What one word do you wish described it?

_____

ASSUMPTIONS—WE ALL HAVE THEM

Imagine you're seated on a subway train, engrossed in your favorite novel, when a woman's screams jerk you out of your book. A large man in a three-piece suit careens past you and leaps through the open doors onto the platform, clutching a baby.

What would you do?

_____

_____

What factors influenced your choice?

_____

_____

Would your reaction change if the man's hair was unkempt and his clothes were tattered?

_____

_____

Are you wondering why we're talking about a man with a baby in a Bible study about Habakkuk? Here's why: To best prepare ourselves to dive into this study about embracing joy, we need to address our assumptions. We all have them, and they affect every area of our lives.

Our life experiences, training, culture, even our temperament and personality feed our assumptions. In turn, our assumptions influence how we interpret all we see and experience, from a man leaping off a subway with a baby to what we read in the Bible.

When we're aware of our assumptions, we have the opportunity to respond to our circumstances, think about our world, and study God's Word with more care and intentionality. The state of our circumstances won't control the state of our hearts.

GOD'S WORD TRANSFORMS

My pastor often says, "God changes lives one verse at a time."

Only God's Word could transform my fear and pride and grow a longing in me for more of His will and less of mine. We're talking about a raise-the-dead miracle. (I'm not where I need to be yet, but praise God, I'm not where I was.)

This is the power of God's Word—resurrection transformation for those who will seek Him in His Word verse by verse.

TRANSFORMATIONAL BIBLE STUDY METHOD

We can apply the truths we learn in Scripture to our lives in many ways, but there's only one correct interpretation of each passage—the one God intended from the beginning. To help us properly interpret Habakkuk and its message—as well as how God wants us to respond to it—we'll use three simple steps.

1. **Intent**—We'll guard against wrong assumptions by considering the author's intent to his original audience.
2. **Truth**—We'll seek to pull out the truths God placed into each verse and what they reveal about the unchanging and unchangeable character, nature, and ways of God and that of anyone or anything else in the passage.
3. **Transformation**—We'll respond to the truths God reveals in His Word in a way that transforms our hearts and minds.

Today and tomorrow, we'll look at the first step: *intent*. We'll cover step two, *truth*, on days three and four. Finally, we'll look at the exciting third step, *transformation*, in our fifth lesson.

STEP ONE: INTENT

The first question we want to keep in mind as we read the Bible is:

What was the author's intent to his original audience?

God designed every word in the Bible to fulfill His good intent. But if we jump into it using our twenty-first-century assumptions, we might make it mean something He never intended.

The authors' ancient writing styles don't always make sense to our modern minds. Context matters. As we prepare to read a book of the Bible, let's consider the following:

- **Historical Context:** What was happening in history when the book was written? Was Israel living in captivity or were they free? Was the book written before or after Christ's resurrection?

Habakkuk was written about six hundred years before Christ. The kingdom of Judah was free but ruled by wicked kings who led them to forsake God, chase after other gods, and commit violence against their own people.

- **Cultural Context:** Societies morph and vary. What one culture considers normal might horrify another. Keep the original audience's culture in mind.

In Habakkuk, his audience—the nation of Judah—should have embraced God's laws, which called for justice, mercy, and faithfulness. Instead, like the surrounding nations, they embraced greed, violence, and every sort of evil behavior.

- **Grammatical and Literary Style:** The Bible's authors wrote to audiences who understood their idioms, lingo, and writing styles. They can baffle us.

How does the grammar affect the meaning of the passage? Is the word *you* singular or plural? Was God speaking to Habakkuk or the whole nation? What's the verb tense? Was the author referring to something Christ has *already* done or is *going* to do?

What type(s) of literature did the author use? Did he write a letter, historical narrative, poem, prophecy, or parable? Most books contain more than one literary style. Habakkuk used poetry, prophecy, and dialogue.

- **Biblical Context:** The Bible is one overarching story of God's redemption through Christ. We want to understand how the book we're reading fits into the whole story.

Habakkuk gives us a dramatic understanding of the gospel. We see man's inability to conquer sin, God's promise of redemption in Christ, and Christ's final judgment.

No matter what we face, we can rest knowing all things belong and fit within the context that God set before time—the context of Jesus Christ, our Savior and Redeemer. He existed before all time, and in Him all things hold together (Colossians 1:17). But this doesn't mean our legs will never tremble when we face challenges.

LET ME WARN YOU

I want to prepare you for God's message through Habakkuk. It's hard. More accurately, it's terrifying. Indignation may rise in you on behalf of God's people, followed by confusion—the same indignation and confusion that tormented Habakkuk.

How could God let such evil fall upon His children? Even more, how could He willingly bring it upon them?

Consider our scenario again. If you watched the man rip the baby from the screaming woman's arms, how would this influence your view of him?

_____

_____

What if you discovered the screaming woman was a kidnapper, and the man was the baby's father? That he was rescuing his child? How would you view him now?

_____

_____

Knowing the man's intent—to save his beloved child—leads us to rejoice rather than panic. Without knowing each person's intent, we analyze situations based on our senses and assumptions. If we knew this man's intent from the beginning, we could help—or at least stay out of his way.

When trouble crashes in, our ability to see (or at least trust) God's intent enables us to rejoice and rest in God rather than panic (Romans 8:28). He's our loving Father. God always accomplishes what He intends—and what He intends is always good and right.

When the truths in God's Word (rather than our emotions or experiences) form our assumptions, we have the right lens through which we can properly interpret the world, our lives, and the Bible.

What situations cause you to clench your fists today? What robs you of sleep? Write down the areas in your life that tempt you to complain, argue, or rage against God.

_____

_____

_____

_____

_____

What assumptions might you bring into your situation that could interfere with your ability to see God's intentions? Do you know very little about God? Have you been betrayed? Do you struggle with trust? (You may need to ask a trusted friend. We're often blind to our own weaknesses or biases.)

_____

_____

_____

_____

FROM QUESTIONS TO EXCLAMATIONS OF PRAISE

If you're hurting right now, you probably don't want to stop and think about intent or assumptions. You just want answers. You want relief. I understand. Habakkuk understood too. He opened his book with a heart-wrenching *Why?* But take heart because we're going to do the same life-changing study Habakkuk did, and his book closes with an exclamation of praise, not despair.

Habakkuk gives us the path to joy. Not a portal to a "better" reality. But if we follow the prophet's steps, we'll wind up where he did—in joyful praise to the God of our salvation no matter our circumstances.

Assumptions drive our reactions.

Read Habakkuk. Don't panic. It's just three chapters. As you read, keep in mind the first question in our Bible study method: What was the author's intent to his original audience? (In other words, lay aside your twenty-first-century assumptions, and enter into this story with a curiosity about that time and place in history.)

Write a prayer asking God to open your eyes to see and understand the truths in Habakkuk. Ask Him to reveal any assumptions you might have that would lead you to form faulty conclusions about God, Habakkuk, or your circumstances. End by thanking Him for sending Christ to save us and making our joy complete (John 15:11).

_____

_____

_____

_____

_____

MEMORY VERSE

Recite this week's memory verse aloud five times.

> For the earth will be filled
>   with the knowledge of the glory of the LORD
>   as the waters cover the sea.

—HABAKKUK 2:14

> **I am the LORD; that is my name; my glory I give to**
> **no other, nor my praise to carved idols.**
>
> —ISAIAH 42:8

Names can be hard to live up to.

Judah means "to praise." The kingdom of Judah failed to live up to their name. They lifted shame, not praise. They rejected God and His Word and committed violence against their own brothers.

Habakkuk, on the other hand, displayed many aspects of his name. *Habakkuk* means "to embrace" or "the embracer." I doubt his parents knew when they named him that someday he'd embrace God's terrifying judgment in one of the most devastating times in Judah's history. Or that he'd embrace Judah as a loving father embraces his rebellious child. He grieved over their sin, but he loved them and longed for them to turn from their evil and return to the Lord. For God to revive the hearts of His people.

Yesterday you read all three chapters of Habakkuk. (You did, right?) How did you feel about God's promise to send an evil nation to sweep through Judah with violence?

_____

If all you knew about God came from the book of Habakkuk, what words would you use to describe Him?

_____

To best understand Habakkuk's message—and how Judah got into such a mess—let's ride a bullet train through Judah's history.

GOD CREATED, MAN CORRUPTED

In the beginning, God created the heavens and the earth—and Adam and Eve corrupted it. They rebelled against Him and ushered sin into the world and into humanity's spiritual DNA.

Sin made us enemies of God and set our hearts to steal, kill, and destroy—all of which humankind quickly mastered.

But God promised Adam and Eve a Savior, Christ the Lord, would come to redeem His children from the penalty and power of sin and death.

Humankind multiplied and flooded the world with every sort of evil. So God flooded the world with water as judgment. But He kept His promise and preserved Noah and his family in the ark. He established a covenant of amazing grace.

A CHOSEN NATION

Later, God called Abraham out of an idol-worshipping nation and made an unconditional and everlasting covenant with him (Genesis 17:7). Through Abraham, God would create a new nation to display how sinful people could live in the presence of a holy God without being struck down for their sin. (The penalty for sin is death, after all—Romans 6:23.)

God promised to give His people a land of their own and to send the Savior through them—specifically through Abraham's son Isaac.

Isaac had two sons—twins. Esau treated God's promises as less valuable than a bowl of stew. Jacob cheated to get what God had already promised before his birth—the younger would rule the older. (Esau was born a minute or two earlier.)

Jacob's twelve sons proved sin is bound up in the heart of even our most precious darlings. Ten of them sold their brother Joseph into slavery in Egypt. But what they intended for evil, God intended for good.

God raised Joseph out of a pit and prison of betrayal and raised him to power in Egypt. He saved his family—even his wretched brothers—from a famine and preserved the line of Christ.

Then Egypt enslaved them. For four hundred years.

A DELIVERER

Through ten terrible plagues and a dramatic parting of the Red Sea, God's prophet Moses led Israel out of slavery.

God dwelled among His people and led them into the promised land. He gave them His law, which overflowed with extravagant blessings if they obeyed and terrifying curses if they rebelled.

Only sin can account for Israel's choice.

They loved their sin more than God's blessings.

In the promised land, everyone did what was right in their own eyes, including sacrificing children to fake gods, human trafficking, slaughtering the innocent, and at least two cases of evil so heinous I can't write about them.

They rejected God and suffered judgment. When the pain became too much, they repented. God raised up a deliverer and restored them into His love.

They repeated this pattern continuously. They loved their sin.

A KING

Israel wanted to be like all the cool nations and have a human king. They didn't want to be ruled by the omnipotent Creator of the universe who delights to shower them with every blessing. They preferred someone limited and selfish.

God gave them a man after their own heart—tall, handsome, and prideful King Saul.

God chose David, a young shepherd boy with a heart after His own.

But even perfect David wasn't perfect. He committed adultery and murder among other sins.

His descendants made evil the norm.

God divided the twelve tribes into two kingdoms. Benjamin and Judah became the southern kingdom of Judah—Habakkuk's audience.

The other ten tribes made up the northern kingdom of Israel.

Both kingdoms embraced evil more than God.

MANY WARNINGS

God sent prophets to warn Judah and Israel to repent and return to Him. Only a few kings in Judah listened to and obeyed the warnings. None in Israel did.

Read 2 Chronicles 36:15–16 and list why God sent messengers.

_____

_____

How did Judah and Israel respond?

_____

_____

For more than two hundred years God sent prophets (including Habakkuk) to warn His people to repent and return to Him or disaster would come.

But they loved their sin and refused His righteous rule.

So God brought down the curses He'd promised.

In 722 BC, God sent Assyria to take Israel into captivity.

In 586 BC, God sent the dreaded and fearsome Babylonians to conquer Judah. They destroyed God's temple and dragged Judah into captivity.

WHY DO WE NEED TO KNOW ALL THIS?

We need to know the backstory of God's people because if we read Habakkuk (and the Old Testament) without understanding the context of humankind's nature and history, we may wrongly accuse God of evil.

We covered more than three thousand years of Judah's history in a few pages, and I greatly limited and softened the accounts of their relentless evil.

The Bible's authors didn't exaggerate the historical events or choose words to incite an emotional frenzy. They reported events without passion, which often made the worst accounts almost palatable. Almost.

Moses reported the world's first murder with zero emotion: "Cain rose up against his brother Abel and killed him" (Genesis 4:8).

Void of emotional verbiage, it could almost appear as if Cain had a valid case when he accused God of judging him too harshly.

With the Bible's just-the-facts reporting style, it's easy to skim past the evil and remain unaffected. Then we read that God destroyed an entire nation, and we're horrified. But if the Bible's authors had recorded the vivid details of the nation's evil, we'd breathe a sigh of relief when God judged them, not shake our fists at Him when He did.

CONTEXT MATTERS

As we read Habakkuk (and the Bible), let's guard against drawing conclusions that are inconsistent with God's character.

Habakkuk witnessed Judah's evil up close. He prayed for God to judge them and wrestled with why God, the Holy One, allowed the evil to continue. But when God answered him, Habakkuk responded like we do. "Wait! That's too harsh."

When we don't get what we want—or we get what we feared—we often overlook the full context and simply react to our emotions.

Horror gripped Habakkuk over God's coming judgment. But he kept it in the context of who God is. He knew he could trust what God was doing in the present—and would do in the future—because of what He'd done in the past.

Context matters.

Read Habakkuk 1. How does understanding the context for God's judgment on Judah change your reaction to His prophecy to Habakkuk?

_____

_____

If you're miffed at God over His plan to judge Judah harshly, don't worry. We're only on the second day of an eight-week study. There's great hope and encouragement ahead that will transform our lives if we believe and act on it.

A right view of our present and future starts with understanding how God worked in the past.

Write a prayer asking God to open your eyes to any rebellion lurking in your heart. Ask Him to forgive you for your sins and thank Him for the power to turn from them. And then do it.

_____

_____

_____

_____

If you've never trusted in Christ for salvation, ask Him to give you the faith to believe.

MEMORY VERSE

Write out this week's memory verse: Habakkuk 2:14.

And you will know the truth, and the truth will set you free.

—JOHN 8:32

I have one brother, and he's a good one—except maybe on that day when I was eight years old.

Thirteen-year-old Rob thundered up our staircase doing his best impression of a monster. I beat him to my room, slammed and locked the door behind me, and cowered in the corner.

His ominous footsteps overwhelmed the truth I knew about him. *He's not a monster. He's not a monster.* The worst Rob would do if he broke through the door was tickle me, but fear had won the moment as I succumbed to my imagination.

Read Habakkuk 2.

TRUST THE TRUTH

Habakkuk's fears weren't rooted in imagination but in God's word to him. Real danger would soon bust down Judah's doors. If the Lord didn't restrain Babylon, they'd all die at the end of a sword, spear, or whatever weapon they'd wield. Babylonian war plans did not include tickling. And so Habakkuk prayed and did the one thing that makes all the difference when we face a trial. He fixed his mind on truth.

Habakkuk looked upward beyond his fears and reminded himself of what he knew to be true about God's unchanging nature. Trusting the truth disarms our fears and puts them in their proper place—under God's feet.

STEP TWO: TRUTH

So far, we've discussed step one of the Transformational Bible Study Method and looked at the intent question.

What was the author's intent to his original audience?

Today we'll look at step two—truth—and the question that helps us focus our eyes upward on the One who is the truth.

What truths does the passage reveal about the character, nature, or ways of God?

The more we know some people, the more we don't trust them and will never willingly obey them. But the more we know and believe about God, the more we'll trust Him, and the more faith and obedience will overflow from our hearts.

God has revealed all we need to know about Him in His divinely inspired Word. It's "profitable for teaching, for reproof, for correction, and for training in righteousness" so we may be "complete, equipped for every good work" (2 Timothy 3:16–17).

> **What comes into our minds when we think about God is the most important thing about us.**
>
> A. W. TOZER,
> *THE KNOWLEDGE OF THE HOLY*

Ages ago, God spoke through His prophets, but today He speaks to us through His Son (Hebrews 1:1–2). Since Jesus no longer walks among us, God has given us the Bible and the Holy Spirit as the primary ways we can know Him and grow in our knowledge of Him today (John 14:26; Galatians 4:6; 2 Peter 1:3).

We'll never truly know the God of the Word apart from the Word of God.

I love what one pastor said: "If you don't have a verse, you only have an opinion." All truth originates with God and is proclaimed in His Word. "Your word is truth" (John 17:17).

To know God, know the Word—the whole Word.

And as we study God's Word, let's ask the truth question:

What truths does God's Word reveal about the character, nature, and ways of God?

To see how the answer to this question looks, we'll study the first phrase in Habakkuk 1:12. (We'll study the full verse in a later lesson.)

When we study the Bible, we want to practice *exegesis*, not *eisegesis*. In other words, when we study a verse, we want to pull out of Scripture what God has put into it (exegesis) rather than inject ourselves or our own ideas into His Word (eisegesis).

In the verse chart below, look at the phrase. In the right box, write any word in the verse that displays an aspect of God's character, nature, and ways.

VERSE	TRUTHS ABOUT GOD
¹² Are you not from everlasting, O Lord my God, my Holy One? We shall not die. —HABAKKUK 1:12	

GOD IS EVERLASTING

Every time He introduces himself in His Word with a new name or character trait, He's telling us something about himself He wants us to know—something we need to know.

The word *everlasting* doesn't describe much in our finite world. On earth, everything from people, careers, and sour cream has a beginning and ending date. But God is eternal. He has no beginning or end. He's unchanging and unchangeable. The same is true of His plans and purposes. He doesn't flip-flop between ideas. His are perfect from their eternal inception because He's never working off new information. He's always known everything fully.

From eternity to eternity, God remains the same.

How does understanding God's eternal nature change the way you view the world and your circumstances?

_____

_____

_____

_____

TRUTH CONTROLS THE MONSTERS

When my brother thundered up the stairs, I overreacted because I imagined he was a monster. Once I acknowledged the truth, the truth controlled the monster, which was my fear, not my brother. I stopped being afraid, and he went back downstairs.

Unlike me, God never overreacts or thinks irrationally. He doesn't have mood swings—or moods. In fact, He doesn't have reactions. He responds.

He knew everything we'd ever do before we were born. He responds to our actions out of His omniscience and wisdom. This should comfort us when trouble comes. God already knew it was coming. He set His purposes for it in eternity.

When Judah received the news about their monster, Babylon, terror was a reasonable response. Since Judah had refused to fear God, God would cause them to fear Babylon.

For hundreds of years, Judah had known God's promises of blessings and curses. They can't cry, "Wait, what?" They rejected the truth they knew and imagined they could keep living the lie that God would never hold them accountable for their sin.

But God and His promises never change. He's Yahweh Elohim, the supreme God who made an everlasting covenant with Judah. He would forever be their God, but Judah needed judgment. At the appointed time, He'd restore them into His love and into their land. But first they needed Babylon.

God never allows trauma to touch us for no reason. But trauma is still terrifying. Truth puts our fears in their proper place, but we can only trust the truth we know.

The more we know the truth through God's Word, the more our fears will fall under God's control. The God who disciplines His children but will never leave or forsake us.

> And behold, I am with you always, to the end of the age.
>
> **MATTHEW 28:20**

TRANSFORMATIONAL TRUTH

Truth puts our fears in their proper place, but we can only trust the truth we know.

How willing are you to trust God in your greatest fears today? Even if He doesn't answer you according to your prayers?

NOPE! JUST CAN'T	WANT TO BE WILLING	PERFECTLY WILLING
0	5	10

What's standing in your way of total trust?

_____

_____

How faithful are you to read the Bible every day?

_____

Have you ever read the whole Bible? If not, start today. (If you read all of Habakkuk, you've already completed one book. Congratulations!)

_____

Consider today's lesson and write out a prayer of thanks to God for the eternal truths you know about Him.

_____

_____

_____

_____

_____

MEMORY VERSE

Write out this week's memory verse: Habakkuk 2:14.

The disciple Peter was a man after my own heart—at least the impetuous Peter we see before Pentecost.

Peter was all in. Until he was out.

Like me, Peter was too often all or nothing.

On the evening of the Last Supper, Jesus knelt to wash the disciples' feet. Peter refused. Their culture relegated feet washing to the lowliest servants. Peter wouldn't allow the Son of God to perform this humiliating task for him.

He said, "You shall never wash my feet."

Not even a pinky toe.

Jesus said, "If I do not wash you, you have no share with me."

"Lord, not my feet only but also my hands and my head!" (John 13:1–20).

All or nothing.

After they left the upper room to go to the garden of Gethsemane, Jesus declared to His disciples they'd all soon abandon Him. Peter said, "I will never fall away. . . . Even if I must die with you, I will not deny you!"

Before the rooster crowed that night, Peter denied he knew Jesus three times—with curse words even (Matthew 26:30–35, 69–75).

All or nothing.

How would you describe your natural tendencies? The kind you display when no one is looking, or you "can't help yourself." Are you like all-or-nothing Peter? Do you flip-flop between following hard after Christ and living like you've never heard of Him?

_____

_____

THE TRUTH ABOUT OUR NATURE

God displays the struggle between our new nature and our sin in the book of Habakkuk. (Did you wonder if I'd forgotten we're studying Habakkuk?)

We're all born with a sin nature steeped in pride. Whether we boast of our greatness or focus on our worthlessness, our inborn responses find their roots in pride.

- Satan's pride believed he deserved God's throne.
- Adam and Eve's pride convinced them they could eat what God had forbidden.
- The Jewish leaders' pride rejected their Messiah and nailed Him to a cross.

Our pride lusts after the highest throne and sets itself against God. Our sin nature wants nothing to do with Him. But by God's grace, He makes His children alive and gives us a new nature—one that sets its mind on Christ's glory and delights to do His will.

Meanwhile, sin remains in us and continues to snatch every weapon in its arsenal to oppose God. It rifles through our hurtful habits and secret longings in hopes of bullying our new nature into silence so it can run free (Romans 8:1–11).

If we know the truth about our inborn sin nature, we can better understand why we humans act like we do since birth. Likewise, if Christians understand our new nature in Christ, we're better prepared to stand against sin.

WHO WE TRULY ARE

When we study the Bible, let's ask the truth question that looks inward to who we truly are.

> *What truths does the passage reveal about the character, nature, and ways of Christians, the world, sin, Satan, or anyone or anything else in the passage other than God?*

Look at Habakkuk 2:4 in the chart below. In the right side of the chart, answer the Inward Truth Question:

VERSE	TRUTHS ABOUT US, THE WORLD, SIN, SATAN, AND ANY OTHER CHARACTER
⁴Behold, his [Babylon's] soul is puffed up; it is not upright within him, but the righteous shall live by his faith. —HABAKKUK 2:4	

We'll look deeper at this verse later in the study. Today, we'll simply note the truths we see in the text about anyone other than God.

"[Babylon's] soul is puffed up" means the proud sinner's soul is puffed up with sinful pride, not humble in righteousness. He's not a sinner because he sins; he sins because he is a sinner.

Babylon is a picture of the world apart from Christ—the proud sinner. Unbelievers.

"It is not upright within him" echoes the previous statement. It's not that Babylon (the proud sinner) acts prideful at times. It's that he cannot act any other way. His soul is sinful. There's no righteousness in him.

Knowing these truths, we might write "Babylon" across the top of the chart and under it list "unbelievers" and "proud sinners."

The word "but" reveals a contrast.

Habakkuk contrasts "Babylon" (the proud unbeliever) with "the righteous" (the humble Christian).

> **When you think of what you are, and despair; think also of what he is, and take heart.**
>
> **C. H. SPURGEON,**
> *THE COMPLETE WORKS OF C. H. SPURGEON*

"The righteous shall live by his faith" means Christians live each day by faith in Christ—although not perfectly. Sin no longer rules us, but we haven't lost our ability to sin. All Christians prove this.

To our list, we could add "Righteous" next to "Babylon" and under "Righteous" list "Christians" and "live by faith in Christ."

FOREWARNED IS FOREARMED

Since birth, we happily traipse wherever our evil sin nature leads us. Likewise, Satan gleefully leads us to a smorgasbord of sin. He's had thousands of years of practice at tempting people to doubt and rebel against God. We need to recognize the evil character and ways of our sin nature and of Satan and his demons, so we won't be deceived.

If I know someone baked poison into a brownie, as much as the rich aroma of chocolate calls to me, I won't be tempted to eat them.

Satan and sin are like poisonous brownies. They promise delight but deliver death.

The more we understand their character, nature, and ways, the less we'll fall for their lies. We mustn't be naive about sin or Satan, but let's not obsess over them either. God reigns.

Forewarned is forearmed.

THE TRUTH GIVES IMMOVABLE FAITH

Impetuous Peter battled his old sin nature until Pentecost. After Christ sent His Holy Spirit, Peter transformed into a rock, no longer tossed about by the whims of sin.

Sin still bullied him as it does all people, but by the power of Christ's indwelling Spirit, he stood strong. Not perfect, but strong. Even when Peter's enemies crucified him upside down, he never again denied his Lord.

As Christians, we can be like post-Pentecost Peter and live as a rock of faith. But if we think there's an earthly answer to our fears or longings, we'll waffle like all-or-nothing Peter. We won't fully depend on God or His Word. It's sin's nature to tempt us to turn to the world instead of Christ.

Knowing and believing the truth about God (His character, nature, and ways) and that of anyone or anything else as revealed in His Word empowers us. We can stand firm in the battle and persevere in Christlike faith until the end (Ephesians 6:10–18).

TRANSFORMATIONAL TRUTH

Forewarned is forearmed.

Write out a prayer and ask God to reveal any sins, weaknesses, sinful tendencies, or traits you may be blind to or clinging to (Psalm 139:23–24).

_____

_____

_____

_____

Are you more concerned with pleasing man than God? Do you tend to snap at people when you're tired?

Surrender your all-or-nothing tendencies to God and commit to walking in your new "all-in" nature in Christ.

Write out this week's memory verse: Habakkuk 2:14.

I used to think the Bible was boring, and Christianity was too hard. I'd followed the Lord for years but responded to my circumstances like the rest of the world. When life fell apart, I fell apart. When was Christianity going to kick in and give me the abiding peace and joy the Bible promised?

I was done.

I wasn't done with Christianity because I knew Jesus is the only way to the Father. I was done with trying to be "a good Christian."

By God's grace, I reached for my Bible. After being a Christian for almost twenty-five years, I still hadn't read much of the Old Testament. What if the answer was on one of the pages I'd never read?

I flipped to Genesis 1:1 and cried out to God. "Lord, I don't care anymore about being a good Christian. I just want to know you. Show me you on every page."

Then I read every page.

And I was changed forever.

TRANSFORMING FROM THE INSIDE OUT

The more I saw of God—His character, nature, and ways—the more my heart changed from the inside out. His Word transformed my beliefs and drove my actions. I began to love what God loves and hate what He hates. I no longer had to force myself to read the Bible. I hungered for His Word every day.

Before God's Word got ahold of me, though, I couldn't produce any lasting spiritual fruit. I was kind one minute and a jerk the next. I waffled between peaceful and panicked.

Why couldn't I master the spiritual fruits? What was I doing wrong?

After God's Word began to conquer my will, I realized I'd answered my question with my question. What I was doing wrong was *doing*. I was trying to produce in my life what only Christ could produce in me. What only He can produce in any of us. Christ must do it all—and He does so by His Spirit working through His Word to change our hearts.

We see this difference in Habakkuk and Judah.

Habakkuk believed and loved God above all else, which resulted in a heart yielded to Him despite Babylon's coming terror. Reverent fear of the Lord anchored him in unfailing hope and transformed his dread into praise.

Judah loved their sin above all else—including God.

Any attributes Judah produced that resembled spiritual fruit were hollow and unsatisfying—like plastic fruit. Anyone can act loving when it benefits them, but only God's love is eternal.

Do you struggle to produce lasting fruit? If the fruit you produce seems hollow—or rotten—don't lose heart.

Read John 15:4–5. Fill in the blank: "Apart from me you can do
_____."

If we cut off a branch from a vine and throw it on the ground, how much fruit will it produce? _____

Write out Hebrews 4:12.

_____

_____

_____

_____

God's Spirit and Word are living and active in us. They do surgery in our hearts to cut away any harmful attitudes or motives and make us like Christ.

Apart from God's Word and the Holy Spirit at work in us, no true and lasting fruit will adorn the branches of our lives. Christ transforms us when we know and believe the truth. This is the focus of our final step in the Transformational Bible Study Method.

STEP THREE: TRANSFORMATION

In review, we've set our minds to see Scripture through a biblical lens (intent). We've soaked our hearts and minds in the truths God's Word reveals (truth). Now we're ready for step three, the transformational question.

> *If I truly believe and act on what God has revealed in this passage, how will the motivations and attitudes of my heart transform and my actions be different tomorrow?*

My mentor, Grace, always asked this question at the end of her Bible studies. It gripped me. What does it look like for my heart to be changed if I truly believe? What is the natural overflow of a changed heart?

As I wrote out my answers, I saw an exciting truth. God doesn't promise His Word *can* transform us. He promises it *will*—if we believe and act on it. Our beliefs always result in actions—whether good or bad. What we believe doesn't simply influence our actions. It determines them.

The book of Habakkuk opened with a question mark and ended with an exclamation point of praise because Habakkuk believed God's word and character.

Beliefs and Actions Always Line Up

If we believe and act on what God has revealed in His Word, we'll rest in God's power. I'm not saying that we *can* rest in God's power if we believe. I'm saying we *will* rest in it. Big difference.

Can is about ability. We're able to rest, but it's still possible we'll fret instead.

True faith, however, leads to a natural overflow. When we believe and act on what God's Word has promised, we *will* rest because our faith is rooted in who God is, not in our ability to drum up enough faith.

No matter what we say we believe (or even think we believe), our actions reveal what we truly believe. And what we truly believe determines our response.

Years ago, I heard a pastor share this convicting truth:

Our beliefs always line up with our actions. We'll either change our actions to line up with our beliefs, or we'll change our beliefs to line up with our actions.

We see this truth lived out in Judah and Habakkuk. Judah wanted to worship other gods like the nations around them, so they adjusted their beliefs to allow their sinful behavior. Habakkuk questioned God's decision to bring severe judgment upon Judah for their sin. But his belief in God's holy character led him to change his question into an exclamation of praise.

What does your life reveal about how steadfastly you believe what you know about God?

_____

_____

_____

Belief Doesn't Create Unfeeling Robots

True belief makes us stable, not emotionless. I'm far from perfect, but much of what rattled me before God's Word began its transforming work no longer unsettles my emotions. I still feel. If anything, I feel more. Yet I don't cry as those who have no hope but rather as one overflowing with hope (1 Thessalonians 4:13).

While I rejoice more now, I still cry deep tears of sorrow over evil, death, and being separated from those I love. And I weep with those who weep (Romans 12:15).

Storms, whether conflicts of nature or man, still cause me to tremble. Righteous Habakkuk trembled at the report of Babylon. True belief in God's Word doesn't create machines. It roots our emotions in God so they're not tossed about by our storms (Ephesians 4:14).

But we can't stand on truth we don't know.

Examine your heart. Consider how well you truly know God's character, nature, and ways. List as many of His attributes as you can in ten seconds.

If you listed only one truth, be encouraged. Even one truth about God is enough to hold us in the storms—if we believe and act on it. You're off to a good start. Keep learning. The more truths you know, the stronger you'll stand.

God has promised to sanctify His children—to grow us up spiritually. We'll either choose to sit and learn the truths in God's Word, or He'll eventually send "life" to sit us down because He loves His children.

Transformation Produces Fruitful Joy

God's Spirit tends His children and grows within them a pleasing, albeit imperfect, harvest of spiritual fruit that leads to fruitful joy.

Read 1 Thessalonians 5:23–24. What does God promise to do for us?

In Christ's new kingdom, we'll eat from the Tree of Life, which grows twelve kinds of delectable fruit every month (Revelation 22:2). Through the power of Christ's life and His Word at work in us, every kind of spiritual fruit will adorn our lives today.

He will do it.

Our beliefs determine our actions.

Consider the truths you know and those we've only begun to glean out of Habakkuk—truths about God and us as well as our sin and pride. Then write a response to the following question.

If I truly believe and act on what God has revealed in today's lesson, how will the motivations and attitudes of my heart transform and my actions be different tomorrow?

Pray and confess any areas of unbelief today's lesson revealed. Ask God to open your eyes to understanding and believing His Word, and for Him to empower you by His Spirit to obey and walk in the truth.

MEMORY VERSE

Write out this week's memory verse: Habakkuk 2:14.

Group Study Questions

Take a few minutes to consider these questions prior to your group study. The leader will choose 2 or 3 to discuss during your group time. If there's remaining time, you can discuss more, of course.

• In the first lesson, we considered a subway scenario with a large man and a baby. Share what you would have done in the moment and what assumptions influenced your reaction.

• What type of reactions did the book of Habakkuk draw out of you as you read it? Were you upset with God? With Judah? Did you feel joy or confusion? Explain your answer.

• What are some of your biggest questions and challenges about the book of Habakkuk?

• Did any of your thoughts or emotions concerning Habakkuk change by the end of the week's lessons? If so, in what ways did they change and why?

• Tell about one of your favorite attributes of God.

BREAK UP INTO GROUPS OF TWO OR THREE.

Practice saying your memory verse to each other:

> For the earth will be filled
> with the knowledge of the glory of the LORD
> as the waters cover the sea.
>
> **—HABAKKUK 2:14**

While still in your smaller groups, share the one word that describes the state of your heart and the word you wished described your heart. (See the first questions from day 1.)

Share a prayer request based on this week's lessons and pray together.

WEEK TWO

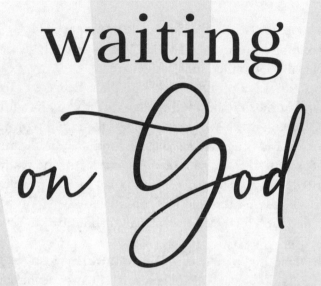

waiting
on God

HABAKKUK 1:1–11

TODAY'S READING

Habakkuk 1:1–2

INTENT

• The book of Habakkuk is an oracle or prophecy (1:1). The Hebrew word for *oracle* means "burden."[2] This certainly describes the weight of Judah's sin and coming judgment.

• Habakkuk was a prophet. God's prophets delivered His word with the same authority as if He'd spoken directly to His audience. The book of Habakkuk is the Word of God, not the ramblings of a man.

Prophets would often *foretell* (tell the future) about events or coming judgment. They'd also *forthtell* (speak forth) the truths the audience needed to hear or declare God's plan for His people.

In Habakkuk, God foretold His coming judgment. Both Habakkuk and God forthtold the truths Judah needed to know and believe.

• Habakkuk used parallelism. (English teachers just got excited. The rest of us said, "What?") Parallelism is a literary device authors use to highlight or reinforce their message.

Parallelism follows a pattern, which can include the following:

- ✦ Repeated words or phrases
- ✦ Opposite thoughts or meanings
- ✦ Synonymous ideas, words, or phrases

For example, note the two synonymous phrases in Habakkuk 2:1: "I will take my stand at my watchpost and station myself on the tower."

• Habakkuk is the only book in the Bible where the dialogue occurs exclusively between the author and God.

• The speakers in Habakkuk change without warning. The content and context reveal who's speaking.

• Habakkuk prays a lament. Biblical laments express God-honoring grief, sorrow, and regret.

TRUTH

"O Lᴏʀᴅ, how long?"

God promised Adam and Eve He'd send a Savior to redeem them from their sin. When Eve cradled Cain, their first child, in her arms, did she think she was looking into the eyes of the Promised One?

Cain was no savior. He was a murderer.

Surely Adam and Eve ached for the Savior as they buried their son Abel, whom Cain killed. But not even their grandchild's grandchild's grandchild would live to see the day Jesus came.

Pain, sorrow, and injustice rip at our hearts today as much as theirs did then.

"O Lᴏʀᴅ, how long shall I cry for help, and you will not hear? Or cry to you 'Violence!' and you will not save?"

Our wise and eternal God is never in a hurry.

And it drives us crazy.

We don't know how long Habakkuk prayed before God broke His silence, but today's reading suggests he'd persisted a long time.

Pray and study Habakkuk 1:1–2 in the chart. Note words or phrases that reveal the character, nature, and ways of God and that of anyone or anything else in the passage.

TRUTHS ABOUT GOD	VERSE	TRUTHS ABOUT OTHERS
	¹ The oracle that Habakkuk the prophet saw.	
	² O Lᴏʀᴅ, how long shall I cry for help, and you will not hear? Or cry to you "Violence!" and you will not save?	

The LORD Is Yahweh

When Habakkuk cried, "O LORD, how long?" he called God *Yahweh*.

"O Yahweh, how long?"

The name Yahweh (literally YHWH in Hebrew) speaks to God's covenant love for His people. This is the name God used for himself to remind His people that He wants to be in relationship with them.

God first introduced His name Yahweh in Genesis 2:4. Before this, He only referred to himself as Elohim—the supreme Creator God, ruler over all (Genesis 1:1).

When God described the details of His fashioning Adam with His hands and breathing life into him, He called himself Yahweh Elohim—our supreme Creator God who loves us with an everlasting love and wants a personal relationship with us (2:4).

Yahweh isn't typically found in English Bibles. Its Hebrew spelling is YHWH but is transcribed in English as LORD. A few English translations of the Bible record YHWH as *Jehovah*. The name YHWH was considered too holy to utter or write.

Soon after God revealed himself in Scripture as Yahweh Elohim, the covenant-keeping Creator, Adam and Eve rebelled against Him. The fact that God chose from before the foundations of the earth to create us (humankind), knowing we'd spurn His love and choose sin over Him, should stagger and humble us.

Read Jeremiah 9:1–9 and list key words that describe some of Judah's sins. Do you see our modern world reflected in Judah?

_____

_____

_____

_____

Out of the Heart the Mouth Speaks

Our words reveal our hearts (Luke 6:45).

What were the first two words out of Habakkuk's mouth when he spoke to God? (See Habakkuk 1:2.)

_____

How could the name Yahweh guide Habakkuk's heart as he prays?

_____

_____

Last week, we discussed our assumptions and the lens through which we view everything. Habakkuk chose to view Judah's circumstances through the lens of God's covenantal name *before* he lifted his despair and confusion to God.

Each of God's names properly exalt Him. The name Yahweh uniquely fixes our minds on His special love for His children.

How can remembering that you pray to Yahweh alter how you interpret your current circumstance?

_____

_____

_____

God Hears Our Laments

It can be hard to pray to a God we can't see, touch, or audibly hear. How much easier would it be if we could look into His kind eyes! Or see Him nod His head in a knowing way that says, "Do not fear. I'm doing a great work."

Habakkuk's anger over Judah's insatiable sin, mixed with his confusion over why God remained silent, led him to cry a prayer of lament—a prayer of deep grief and sorrow.

He wasn't throwing a toddler tantrum when he cried out "Why?"

He didn't walk away from God to look for deliverance elsewhere.

Instead, he bowed himself at the feet of the Holy One and trusted Him alone for deliverance.

Biblical laments are humble cries of sorrow as we live in a world that suffers the devastating consequences of sin. True faith stands strong even in the worst trials, but not with a cold heart.

Read Jesus's lament over Jerusalem in Matthew 23:37.

Jesus's lament didn't display a lack of faith or hopelessness. Instead, it revealed His heart of compassion—even for men who stoned and killed His most faithful servants.

Read 2 Peter 3:9–10. Why is God "slow" in answering His people's prayers for Christ's return?

_____

_____

Read Ezekiel 33:11. Who is lamenting in this verse? And why?

_____

_____

We struggle to wait five minutes, much less five years, for God to fulfill His good purposes for us. Only He knows the right timing for every action under heaven.

The thought of loved ones standing condemned before the judgment seat of God makes me weak with deep sorrow. Would you joyfully wait fifty years for God to answer your deepest prayer if you knew it would result in the salvation of all those you love?

Wait on the Lord. He hears and cares.

Trust God's Eternal Timeline

Jesus is our perfect example of trusting God's eternal timeline. Like His Father, Jesus was never in a hurry.

- Jesus came into the world about four thousand years after God's promise to send the Savior (Genesis 3:15). He waited for His appointed time.
- Jesus came as a baby. It took a calendar, not a clock, to watch for Jesus's public ministry to begin. (It began at age thirty.)
- The Jewish leaders tried more than once to seize and kill Jesus, but Jesus continued to minister freely. No one could lay a hand on Him until His hour had come (John 7:30, 44).

God's answers to our trials will arrive at their ordained time by His hand, not through our forcing a premature resolution.

Pray with patient persistence, and walk in obedience to God's Word and His leading while you wait. And keep this truth in mind: When we wait on God, we wait on our wise, eternal, and promise-keeping Yahweh Elohim who hears our laments and cares. He's on the move.

TRANSFORMATION

Jesus is our Amen. *Amen* means "firm" and "faithful."[3] When used at the beginning of a statement, it means "surely" and "truly." When used at the end, it means, "So it is, so be it, may it be fulfilled."[4] Jesus is our faithful Amen. He will fulfill all His Word and all His purposes. But He won't be in a hurry. He'll be right on time.

Write out Revelation 22:20–21. These are Jesus's final words to us until we see Him face-to-face.

Our wise and eternal God is never in a hurry.

Consider the transformation question below and write a prayer of response to today's reading. Use the name Yahweh in your prayer and end it with *amen*.

> *If I truly believe and act on what God has revealed in this passage, how will the motivations and attitudes of my heart transform and my actions be different tomorrow?*

MEMORY VERSE

Recite this week's memory verse aloud five times.

Look among the nations, and see;
wonder and be astounded.
For I am doing a work in your days
that you would not believe if told.

—HABAKKUK 1:5

TODAY'S READING

Habakkuk 1:3–4

INTENT

- Habakkuk is talking to God about Judah's evil and violence toward their own brothers.

TRUTH

Deep within the barbed wire confines of Ravensbrück, a Nazi concentration camp, two Dutch watchmakers—Corrie ten Boom and her sister, Betsie—ached to see God move. Surrounded by unimaginable evil, questions swirled in their hearts. Why did God allow such wickedness to flourish?

When fleas covered their cramped barracks, Corrie despaired. But not Betsie. She looked on the vile insects as a gift, not an added trial. The bloodsucking varmints drove the cruel guards away and gave them a measure of relief from the guards' torment.

Betsie didn't doubt God even when the trials grew worse. She doubted her doubts.

Would Habakkuk doubt God in the face of the evil he witnessed in Judah? Or would he doubt his doubts?

Pray and study Habakkuk 1:3–4 in the chart. Note words or phrases that reveal the character, nature, and ways of God and that of anyone or anything else in the passage.

TRUTHS ABOUT GOD	VERSE	TRUTHS ABOUT OTHERS
	³ Why do you make me see iniquity, and why do you idly look at wrong? Destruction and violence are before me; strife and contention arise.	
	⁴ So the law is paralyzed, and justice never goes forth. For the wicked surround the righteous; so justice goes forth perverted.	

What We See versus What We Know

If we detailed all Judah's sins, it wouldn't pass Christian publishers' guidelines for what's fit for printing. God promised His people overflowing blessings and security in the promised land if they obeyed His Word and rejected the heinous sins of the people who lived in the land before them.

Read 2 Kings 21:9. What did God say His people did?

_____

In 2 Kings 21, God chronicled some of the sins King Manasseh led Judah to commit with words like *evil*, *despicable*, and *abominations*. He wasn't wrong. Manasseh burned his own son as an offering to a foreign god (v. 6).

Let that sink in.

What emotions rose in you?

Manasseh reigned fifty-five years. He repented before his death, but the devastation from the violence, strife, and contention he poured out on Judah was irreversible.

Do we understand Habakkuk's lament better?

How many of us could witness such atrocities and not be tempted to doubt God?

What we *see* can blind us to what we *know*.

What does God's Word tell us we can know about God's character? Write out the verses and create a bullet point list of Truths about God in the chart.

VERSE	TRUTHS ABOUT GOD
Psalm 18:30	
Psalm 116:5	

How will remembering these truths help you the next time you're tempted to doubt God?

_____

_____

_____

_____

Ignoring God's Word Leads to Destruction

God's Word is perfect and without error in the original language. And it declares that God is perfect in His character, nature, and ways (Matthew 5:48).

To doubt God is to doubt His Word and thus reject it.

Habakkuk showed us the progression sin takes when we reject or ignore God's Word (law).

So the law is paralyzed, and justice never goes forth. For the wicked surround the righteous; so justice goes forth perverted. (Habakkuk 1:4)

Fill in the blanks for the progressive consequences of sin:

1. When we ignore God's Word (law), justice _____
2. When justice doesn't go forth, the wicked _____
3. When the wicked surround the righteous, justice _____

Did you notice statements 1 and 3 seem to contradict themselves? The law of contradiction says something can't be both true and untrue within the same context. Why do you think both statements are true?

_____

_____

_____

God determines justice, not man. Our sin nature perverts justice and creates a distorted imitation that isn't justice at all. It's only our twisted idea of justice.

The world's way leads to perversion and destruction, like Judah committing violence against their own brother and God's people nailing His Son to the cross.

God's ways lead to justice and righteousness, like Christ humbling himself "by becoming obedient to the point of death, even death on a cross" (Philippians 2:8). In His death, Christ satisfied God's righteousness, justice, and mercy—and He purchased our freedom from sin.

Never Forget to Remember

When evil thrives, many professing Christians abandon God. They accuse Him of either being guilty of abuse or gross negligence or being too weak to stop the violence.

Was Habakkuk blaming God in verse 3?

Habakkuk wouldn't be the first prophet to express anger at Him. Jonah grumbled against God when the city of Nineveh repented of their evil and God showed them mercy.

Read Jonah 4:1–4.

List some traits Jonah confessed about God. (See verse 2.)

_____

Like Jonah, Habakkuk questioned God's allowing evil. He could either doubt God or doubt his doubts.

Which path did Jonah take? (See verse 3.)

_____

How did God respond? (See verse 4.)

_____

Read Jonah 4:5–11 and circle below where Jonah's anger led him.

- The peace of God ruling his heart

- Outbursts of self-pity

When our circumstances tempt us to doubt God, let's call to mind the truth we know about the Lord and stand on it. Jonah knew the truth, but he sat and whined.

Even humble Job buckled a little under heavy pressure. He knew the truth, but his physical agony led him to see God as his enemy (Job 6:4). But then God took him on a stunning four-chapter dissertation on who He is. His words led Job to repent in dust and ashes (Job 38–41; 42:1–6).

How often are we like Job and Jonah and let our circumstances and emotions dictate truth? Habakkuk wasn't wrong about God allowing Judah to continue their violence, but he was close to accusing God of wrongdoing.

Pain and sorrow have blinding power.

Christians have the power that raised Christ from the dead.

The Holy Spirit empowers us to demand our emotions surrender and submit to the truth. To give truth its rightful reign in our hearts and minds.

What does God call us to do in 2 Corinthians 10:5?

_____

_____

Think on the situations in your life that could feed your doubts. Underline how you're more likely to respond:

- "Why is God doing this to me?"

- "I wonder what God is up to. Whatever it is, it will ultimately serve my good."

How might God be using your current challenges—as hard as they may be—to bless you in the end? (Spiritual blessings are the greatest.)

_____

_____

What tendencies do you have that might fuel your doubts? Because of your past, do you tend to assume people are against you? Have you suffered many losses and fear God will take even more away from you? Were you raised by a single parent and tend to doubt God's faithfulness?

_____

_____

_____

_____

Start a list of truths from Scripture that can help relieve these doubts—and add to it often.

_____

_____

_____

_____

TRANSFORMATION

Jesus is Immanuel, God with us (Matthew 1:22–23). The world may betray us and walk out on us, but Christ never will. God in flesh came into the world to dwell among us. And He promised never to leave or forsake us (Hebrews 13:5). To be with us always (Matthew 28:20).

Betsie ten Boom could've doubted God continually as she lived surrounded by pure evil. Instead, she kept her eyes on the truth—on Christ. In December 1944, Betsie took ill and died. Corrie described Betsie's face as peaceful. Such is the power of Christ in the heart of His children.

Twelve days later, Corrie walked out of Ravensbrück. Officials released her due to a clerical error (we know it as the hand of God). Ten days after they freed her, the Nazis sent every woman in Corrie's age group to the gas chambers.

> Lord, I believe; help my unbelief!
>
> MARK 9:24 (NKJV)

God rescued both Betsie and Corrie. His ways and timing were different for both, but His love and faithfulness remained the same.

Corrie spent the rest of her life following Betsie's example. She chose to doubt her doubts, not God.

Doubt your doubts, not God.

Consider the truths in Habakkuk 1:3–4 and write a response to the following question.

If I truly believe and act on what God has revealed in this passage, how will the motivations and attitudes of my heart transform and my actions be different tomorrow?

_____

_____

Pray and confess any areas of unbelief today's reading revealed. Ask God to open your eyes to understanding and believing His Word, and for Him to empower you by His Spirit to obey and walk in the truth.

MEMORY VERSE

Write out this week's memory verse: Habakkuk 1:5.

TODAY'S READING

Habakkuk 1:5–6

INTENT

- The speaker changed. God is now answering Habakkuk's cries.
- Habakkuk questioned as an individual. God answered to a plurality. God didn't say, "Look, Habakkuk." He said, "Look, you all." (Or, as we say in the South, "All y'all.") But who was the all y'all? Most believe it's the kingdom of Judah.
- Chaldeans is another name for Babylonians.

TRUTH

Mr. Wonderful, the most popular guy in high school, invited me for a ride after school. We'd been dating about a month. At the top of Kennesaw Mountain, we sat on the hood of his car and admired the view.

He said, "I want to tell you why I invited you here."

My heart fluttered.

"I think we should see other people."

The magnitude of disappointment between what I expected him to say ("I love you") to what he actually said ("We're done") barely ripples the ocean of Habakkuk's disappointment. I struggled to hold back tears. Habakkuk struggled to hold back terror.

Pray and study Habakkuk 1:5–6 in the chart. Note words or phrases that reveal the character, nature, and ways of God and that of anyone or anything else in the passage.

TRUTHS ABOUT GOD	VERSE	TRUTHS ABOUT OTHERS
	⁵ Look among the nations, and see; wonder and be astounded. For I am doing a work in your days that you would not believe if told.	
	⁶ For behold, I am raising up the Chaldeans, that bitter and hasty nation, who march through the breadth of the earth, to seize dwellings not their own.	

It's All about Him

God's purpose in history is to work out the mystery of His will—Christ redeeming His children and uniting all things in himself in the fullness of time for His glory. It's a grand story with billions of threads, and each thread matters. Each is connected and woven into the central thread—Christ.

It's all about Him.

But sin tempts us to make the story about us and to demand control over the threads according to our desires.

I would never have included the thread of my mom dying of cancer or my dad developing dementia. We all have a picture of what constitutes good and right, but how can we know better than God?

We can only know what we've learned, seen, or experienced. God, on the other hand, knows all things. He doesn't just know truth. He is the Truth.

His Word is our only trustworthy authority for truth.

I thought Mr. Wonderful in high school was good and right for me. I'm glad he (and God) disagreed. I would've missed out on my husband, Larry, and our wonderful children and grandchildren.

> Who is this that darkens counsel by words without knowledge?
>
> **JOB 38:2**

Share about a time you *knew* something was good and right, only to learn later you were wrong.

What We Expect versus What We Need

If you were Habakkuk, imagine what might go through your mind when God basically said, "Be prepared, Habakkuk and Judah. I'm about to blow your minds" (v. 5).

List some emotions God's words in verse 5 might evoke if you were Habakkuk.

My heart would probably have soared with anticipation. Is God about to do a part-the-Red-Sea-and-rescue-His-people kind of work? God often raised up a savior to rescue His people. Not today, Habakkuk. God was doing something different. He was raising up what Judah didn't expect . . . but needed.

In one sentence God's message went from sounding like "I love you" to "We're done." Habakkuk's cry went from "O LORD, how long?" to "Whoa, Lord. Slow down. Can we talk about this? How can this plan be good?"

In infinite wisdom, God knows exactly what we need—and He's always right.

In sovereign power, He's able to bring about His good purposes in every life—all at the same time.

Wrestle with God's Plan, Not His Character

When we face unexpected (and unwelcome) moments, we're invited to come to Him with our questions, concerns, and confusions. Wrestling with God's plans fosters humble searching. Wrestling with God's character fosters unbelief.

For years I wrestled with God's use of pain in our lives. (Mine particularly.) Why would the God of the universe who can do all things sometimes choose pain to move us? Why can't He always use kindness and blessings? The questions tortured me. I kept seeking until I found the answer.

The answer isn't what God *can't* do. It's what we *won't* do.

We simply won't always respond to kindness like we'll respond to pain.

It's also what God *will* do. He'll work for the good of those who love him (Romans 8:28). He'll use every circumstance, even the ones we don't like or expect, to accomplish His purposes, which will result in the praise of His glory and our ultimate joy.

Will we believe?

Read Luke 1:5–38.

What did Zechariah say in verse 18?

_____

What did Mary say in verse 34?

_____

What's the difference between Zechariah's and Mary's questions?

_____

_____

How did Gabriel respond to Zechariah's question (vv. 19–20)?

_____

How did Gabriel respond to Mary's question (v. 35)?

_____

Write Mary's response to Gabriel's answer (v. 38).

_____

What did Zechariah say in response to Gabriel's answer?

_____

That last one was a trick question. Zechariah couldn't speak until he announced his newborn son's name: "His name is John" (v. 63).

God Honors Curiosity, Not Unbelief

The difference between Zechariah's and Mary's responses came down to *curiosity* and *unbelief*.

Zechariah didn't question *how* Elizabeth would have a baby. Zechariah and Elizabeth were married. They knew how God gives babies and that God can open dead wombs. (Remember Abraham and Sarah.) Instead, Zechariah questioned how he could *know* it would happen. The answer should have been obvious—by believing the angel God sent.

Despite the joyous news Zechariah received, he wrestled with God's character, not with understanding His plan. He doubted God's power to give Elizabeth a baby at her old age and His faithfulness to fulfill His Word.

On the other hand, Mary was engaged, not married. She knew babies didn't come from virgins. Despite the dangerous position God was placing her into as an unwed mother in her culture, Mary didn't doubt God. She wrestled with understanding the details of His plan, but not with Him or His character. She believed God was good and right in all He does and able to do the impossible. She simply had no clue how such a thing *would*—not *could*—happen.

TRANSFORMATION

Jesus is faithful. Life is full of unexpected disappointments, but Jesus is faithful. Why should our hope ever waver that He's working out what concerns us according to His own wise counsel? He never disappoints.

Write out Hebrews 10:23.

Before I sat down to write this week's lessons, I wrote a eulogy for one of my best friends. God gave me what I didn't want. What none of Billie Jo's family or friends wanted.

I'll still cry over missing Billie Jo as I learn to live without sitting in the sunshine together each week and talking about all that we loved—and a few things that drove us crazy. I don't know why it was best for Billie Jo to go home to heaven now rather than in her old age, but I trust Him. Wrestling with Christ's faithfulness only leads to fear and doubt.

Whenever life feels like a bitter and hasty nation has seized your joy, cry out to God. Ask Him questions. Lots of them. But don't wrestle with His flawless character. Instead, remind yourself of His unfailing attributes. Keep a growing list of them at your fingertip and whip them out whenever fear or sorrow threaten you.

God's ways are always good and unfailing. They just don't always feel good. But when we fix our eyes on the Lord and on His Word, we'll find that the Truth will never fail us.

Did you lose your job? Get passed over for a promotion?

Did the doctor tell you he can't find your baby's heartbeat?

Did you write a loved one's eulogy?

Trust the Faithful One, even if He brings what feels more like "We're done" than "I love you."

Wrestling with God's plans fosters humble searching. Wrestling with God's character fosters unbelief.

Consider the truths in today's reading and write a response to the following question.

If I truly believe and act on what God has revealed in this passage, how will the motivations and attitudes of my heart transform and my actions be different tomorrow?

Pray and confess any areas of unbelief today's reading revealed. Ask God to open your eyes to understanding and believing His Word, and for Him to empower you by His Spirit to obey and walk in the truth.

MEMORY VERSE

Write out this week's memory verse: Habakkuk 1:5.

TODAY'S READING

Habakkuk 1:7–8

INTENT

• God continues to describe the dreaded and proud Babylonians and their swift conquest.

TRUTH

"Don't make Me count to ten."

These weren't God's words, but they were implied when He sent Moses to tell Pharaoh, "Let my people go" (Exodus 7:16).

From blood in the Nile River to blood around Israel's doors, God gave Pharaoh ten chances to humble himself and obey. Despite the devastating plagues, Pharaoh refused to bow his will to God's.

"But God wasn't fair to Pharaoh," I've heard many say. "He hardened Pharaoh's heart. Pharaoh didn't have a choice" (see Exodus 10:20).

Just as soft clay hardens when removed from its protective covering and left in the sun, so Pharaoh's heart was hardened when God removed His restraining hand. Pharaoh chose his sin, and only God's protection kept him from heaping even worse evil on God's people.

For the most part, God had turned Pharaoh over to his own sin-encrusted heart to do what he wanted. God removed Pharaoh's choice only when He forced him to let Israel go. Pharaoh was already bent on rebelling against God and positioning himself as the highest authority in the universe. Even though Pharaoh suffered along with his people with each plague, he refused to submit to God.

Pharaoh's pride blinded him to the truth that his rebellion was destroying his country.

His servants saw it and begged Pharaoh to let God's people go (Exodus 10:7).

After God forced Pharaoh to release His people, Pharaoh again followed his unquenched pride. He set off with his army on horses and chariots to drag Israel back into captivity.

Like Babylon's army, their horses were swifter than leopards and fiercer than wolves. Their horsemen pressed proudly on. They flew like eagles swift to devour. But God devoured Pharaoh and his army instead (12:29; 14:5–31).

Pharaoh learned the inescapable truth. We can choose our sin, but God chooses the consequences.

Pray and study Habakkuk 1:7–8 in the chart. Note words or phrases that reveal the character, nature, and ways of God and that of anyone or anything else in the passage.

TRUTHS ABOUT GOD	VERSE	TRUTHS ABOUT OTHERS
	7 They are dreaded and fearsome; their justice and dignity go forth from themselves.	
	8 Their horses are swifter than leopards, more fierce than the evening wolves; their horsemen press proudly on. Their horsemen come from afar; they fly like an eagle swift to devour.	

Choose Well

Judah's sins were as rebellious as Pharaoh's; nevertheless, when Habakkuk heard God declare their consequences, his knees nearly buckled.

But Judah was without excuse.

Moses left a written account of God's mighty works in Egypt and in the wilderness. He detailed the blessings the Lord would pour out on them if they followed Him—as well as the curses if they refused.

The list filled three chapters (Deuteronomy 28–30).

At the end of the list, Moses gave Israel choices.

Read Deuteronomy 30:19–20 and write down the choices Israel was given.

_____

_____

History reveals what they chose.

Their pride deluded them into believing they'd never really have to pay the consequences of rebelling against God and chasing after idols.

Judah knew better.

Habakkuk 1:8 mirrors one of the curse verses in Deuteronomy 28:49, "The Lord will bring a nation against you from far away, from the end of the earth, swooping down like the eagle, a nation whose language you do not understand."

Judah made an informed decision. They knew the truth but chose their sin. But God chose their consequences.

Welcome to Babylon!

Babylon's pride and arrogance knew no end. They marched across the earth as judge, jury, and executioner without remorse or pity. "They are dreaded and fearsome; their justice and dignity go forth from themselves" (Habakkuk 1:7).

And Judah had no one to blame but themselves. God had warned and promised them. Often.

Sin Brings Consequences We Never Imagined

The violence Judah had committed against their own people would now turn back on them with a swiftness and ferocity they couldn't imagine. Such is the cost of sin apart from the restraining hand of God.

Sin touches everything and everyone around us in unexpected ways. If we don't turn from our sins, those we love most could pay the highest cost. May we repent before the cost grows devastatingly steep. May we embrace the mercy and grace of God before He must discipline us . . . and before our loved ones get swept up in our discipline.

Are there any sins you need to repent of? Be ruthless in forsaking sin because sin will be ruthless with you.

Justice and Sovereignty Belong to God

Apart from Christ, pride blinds us to wisdom. And a lack of wisdom leads to foolishness.

Sin paints the truth as a lie and a lie as the truth.

Our pride says to sin, "Okay, I believe you."

Like Pharaoh, King Nebuchadnezzar's inflated pride deluded him into exalting his greatness above all others. Nebuchadnezzar thought he'd raised Babylon from obscurity into an overnight wonder by his own power. Babylon thought justice and sovereignty originated from them, but God alone holds all power and authority (Romans 13:1).

This reminds me of the Jewish leaders and Pilate.

Who did Pilate think held the authority to determine whether Jesus lived or died? (John 19:10)

Who did Jesus say held the authority? (v. 11)

What did Pilate try to do with Jesus? (v. 12)

Pilate found no guilt in Jesus. He offered to release Him, but the crowd demanded the murderer Barabbas be released instead (18:38–40). Pilate again sought to release Jesus but didn't. Ultimately, he handed Him over to be crucified.

Why?

Was it because of the will of the people who cried out for His death?

No. It was because God keeps His promises—including those made thousands of years earlier in the garden of Eden (Genesis 3:15).

Christ came to earth to die on the cross for the sins of the world. Pilate thought his authority sent Jesus to the cross—even though he tried to release Him and couldn't.

The Jewish leaders thought their authority led to Jesus's death—even though they'd tried to kill Him earlier but couldn't (John 8:59; 10:31).

The Babylonians thought they made themselves great. That they were sovereign.

They all thought wrong. Justice and sovereignty belong to God.

TRANSFORMATION

Jesus is our Redeemer (Isaiah 48:17). Each of us is as guilty as Pharaoh, the people of Judah, and even Babylon. We're sinners who love our sin. But the one who trusts in Christ has been set free from sin's punishment. Free of all condemnation. "So if the Son sets you free, you will be free indeed" (John 8:36).

> She will bear a son, and you shall call his name Jesus, for he will save his people from their sins.
>
> **MATTHEW 1:21**

No matter how far sin has taken you, Christ will redeem you. His arm is not too short to reach you wherever you are. Satan wants you to believe it's too late, but Christ is greater than all your sins. Run to Him.

We choose our sin. God chooses the consequences.

Consider the truths in today's reading and write a response to the following question.

If I truly believe and act on what God has revealed in this passage, how will the motivations and attitudes of my heart transform and my actions be different tomorrow?

_____

_____

Pray and confess any areas of unbelief today's reading revealed. Ask God to open your eyes to understanding and believing His Word, and for Him to empower you by His Spirit to obey and walk in the truth.

MEMORY VERSE

Write out this week's memory verse: Habakkuk 1:5.

TODAY'S READING

Habakkuk 1:9–11

INTENT

• Babylon intimidated their enemies with violent military strategies, such as their "ideology of terror," which included "flaying alive, impalement, cutting off body parts and burning alive."[5] (I'd certainly surrender.)

• Ancient seize tactics included piling up earth and stone to create ramps against the city walls to break through the city's defenses.[6]

• Babylon had zero regard for the sovereignty of other nations or kings. They swept through their lands with a I-do-whatever-I-want and a what's-yours-is-mine mentality.[7]

• Scholars aren't certain if verse 11 ascribes Babylon's might to their gods (such as Marduk or Nabu) or proclaims that their own might is their god.[8]

TRUTH

Click.

I didn't need to turn toward the sound to confirm my fears. I knew the click of a door locking.

Panic pierced my soul.

Lord, help me survive. My parents can't wake up to find me dead. I've got to live. I've got to—

Sin Plays Its Game Well

My parents and I were visiting Venice, Italy, when they awakened with the flu. I left them to sleep while I headed out to walk around the city, meet fascinating people, and write in my journal. A predator who played his game well had other plans.

When the twenty-something Italian introduced himself, my guard went up, but he remained casual and nonthreatening. After we talked for a while, he invited me to join him at a restaurant.

Public place. Should be safe.

"Sure. Why not."

We ate and chatted for two hours. He said he worked as a DJ at a radio station.

"Would you like to see it? It's nearby."

Public place. Should be safe.

"Sure. Why not."

When we got to the building, my new friend opened the door and ushered me in. Alarm bells blared in my head.

This doesn't feel like an office building.

Then he led me through another door, flipped on the light, and blinded me with the truth.

This is no radio station. And he is not a friend.

I was standing in the apartment of a rapist.

Click.

Pray and study Habakkuk 1:9–11 in the chart. Note words or phrases that reveal the character, nature, and ways of God and that of anyone or anything else in the passage.

TRUTHS ABOUT GOD	VERSE	TRUTHS ABOUT OTHERS
	⁹ They all come for violence, all their faces forward. They gather captives like sand.	
	¹⁰ At kings they scoff, and at rulers they laugh. They laugh at every fortress, for they pile up earth and take it.	
	¹¹ Then they sweep by like the wind and go on, guilty men, whose own might is their god!	

Who's In Control When Evil Wins?

Alarm bells had gone off in Habakkuk's head for some time as he watched Judah turn from God and embrace evil. But the evil of Babylon would soon eclipse Judah's. They would sweep through with violence, gather bounty and captives like sand, and drag them home. *Click.*

When evil wins (or in truth, seems to win), it's easy for us to imagine—or even wholeheartedly believe—that God is not in control. After all, Scripture tells us that the devil is "ruler of this world" and the "prince of the power of the air" (John 12:31; Ephesians 2:2).

I once heard a pastor preach that God is in charge but not in control. He maintained that the presence of evil proved his point. But Scripture proves otherwise. God does indeed allow Satan power on earth, but God remains forever in control over all—including Satan.

Summarize what the following verses say about God's rule and power.

- Psalm 103:19
- Psalm 115:3
- Proverbs 16:33

The Devil Is God's Devil

Before the beginning of time, Satan served God willingly, but by some mystery, pride filled his heart. He ceased to be God's friend, but he never ceased to be under God's authority. Make no mistake, the devil is a merciless liar and murderer, who tempts us that he may steal, kill, and destroy (Luke 22:31; John 8:44; 10:10; 1 Thessalonians 3:5).

But God remains in control.

Martin Luther said it well: "The devil is God's devil."

Neither sin nor Satan can control, limit, or restrain God. Just as He says to the waves that lap onto the shore, "Thus far shall you come, and no farther," (Job 38:8–11), the Lord controls, restrains, and sets limits on each person's sin and on Satan. If God didn't, no child of His would be alive today. Sin and Satan never voluntarily hold back.

Our sovereign God oversees every moment of our lives with the watchful eye of a loving and almighty Father. We can trust Him for whatever He permits.

Nebuchadnezzar adored his sin. He lived as though he could do whatever he wanted with whoever he wanted for whatever purpose he wanted whenever he wanted. Victory came easily for him because God handed it to him for a limited time. The only reason

Babylon didn't rape, pillage, and destroy all of Judah is because God restrained them.

In time, Nebuchadnezzar learned that God alone rules over all. He alone is sovereign (Daniel 4:25–26). All creation exists and operates under God's authority, not our own.

Babylon is God's Babylon.

All for Good

Ungodly Babylon served God's good purposes for Judah. The cross of Christ served His great purpose for our salvation. God causes all things—the best things and the worst things—to work together for good.

I don't mean God runs after Satan to clean up his messes and tie pretty bows over our pain. I definitely don't mean God condones or overlooks evil. He hates sin. I'm saying God knew from before time that I'd be in Venice and fall prey to a rapist. He also knew He wouldn't let the man kill me but ensure he set me free.

I don't know why God allowed the rape. But He knows and is wholly trustworthy (Psalm 18:30).

He's always known the good He'd work together for me out of the sin He hates (Isaiah 46:9–11).

He's always known the supernatural peace He'd pour into my heart as I prayed, and which miraculously gave me sweet sleep that night (Philippians 4:6–7).

He's always known the strength He'd build into my faith over the years as I battled and overcame PTSD (James 1:2–4). The growing understanding of His perfect love He'd teach me that would cast out the overwhelming fears that had consumed me and affected my marriage and ability to stay home alone, as well as irrational fears over my daughters' safety (1 John 4:18).

God has always known and cared about all my suffering, and that He's working all of it for good to make me more like His Son—full of abiding joy and peace.

Rest in His promise that what He permits, He works out for the good of His children. All else, He restrains.

Read Romans 8:28–29.

In the prayer below, fill in the blank with a current challenge you or a loved one are facing.

Father, as your child, I cling to and thank you for your promise that you cause all things, including _____

_____, to work together for good as part of your kind and wise plan to make me more like your Son. Help me look forward in faith to the abiding peace and joy to come and to embrace them even today through my weakness and tears. Open my eyes to every droplet of good, and refresh me with your presence and love to your great and eternal glory. Amen.

The Guilty Pay

Because our eternal God is never in a hurry, evil often appears like it's winning, but don't be deceived. The guilty get away with nothing.

In mercy, God often uses someone's own evil to lead them to repentance and faith in Him. He saves the most unlikely candidates. But those who refuse will stand before God and receive the judgment for all their evil. "These things you have done, and I have been silent; you thought that I was one like yourself. But now I rebuke you and lay the charge before you" (Psalm 50:21).

God will judge my attacker—if He hasn't already. The guilty all pay.

Before Babylon even conquered Judah, God proclaimed their guilt (Habakkuk 1:11). At the appointed time, God judged Babylon and brought down their empire faster than He raised it. Judah would have to wait seventy years to see the day, but those who trusted in Him and lived by faith saw His goodness each of the 25,550-plus days. That's a lot of goodness.

God said to Judah about their captivity in Babylon, "For I know the plans I have for you, declares the LORD, plans for welfare and not for evil, to give you a future and a hope" (Jeremiah 29:11).

Babylon was evil, but God's plans for His people in Babylon were good.

It was all for good.

In the fullness of time, all evil will end (Revelation 20:10). Until then, walk by faith and remember that God is holding you each step of the way.

Meditate on Psalm 73:25–28. Summarize what the passage reveals about the fate of evil and the great hope for those who take refuge in Him.

On Christ the Solid Rock I Stand

After I made it back to my room that night, I sobbed on my bed and listened to the hymn, "On Christ the Solid Rock I Stand." Over and over.

Darkness had veiled God's lovely face, but the more the truth of the words in the hymn washed over my tormented soul, the more I rested on His unchanging grace.

I'd endured the highest and stormiest gale, but Christ, my anchor, held me within His veil as I drifted off to sleep. On Christ the solid rock I stand—and sleep.

Years before, God had saved my soul. That night He'd saved my life. And now, for the first time, I knew what it really meant to have nothing but Christ. I'd nearly despaired of life much less of anything else, but the Lord never left me, and I found what Habakkuk knew and believed: The Lord is enough.

As inhabitants of earth, we've all endured evil, but some of you have endured unspeakable darkness. My heart breaks for you. Even more, Christ's heart breaks for you.

Whether your suffering came at the hands of evil or a natural tragedy, I pray you'll come to know and believe that Christ is your solid rock. He will never fail you—and Satan can never have you.

What evil is tormenting your soul today? Consider the words of the great hymn "On Christ the Solid Rock I Stand." Let the promises of God's Word and His Spirit comfort and strengthen you today. He will hold you fast.

On Christ the Solid Rock I Stand

My hope is built on nothing less
Than Jesus Christ, my righteousness;
I dare not trust the sweetest frame,
But wholly lean on Jesus' name.

On Christ, the solid Rock, I stand;
All other ground is sinking sand,
All other ground is sinking sand.

When darkness veils His lovely face,
I rest on His unchanging grace;
In every high and stormy gale,
My anchor holds within the veil.

His oath, His covenant, His blood,
Support me in the whelming flood;
When all around my soul gives way,
He then is all my hope and stay.

When He shall come with trumpet sound,
Oh, may I then in Him be found;
In Him, my righteousness, alone,
Faultless to stand before the throne.

TRANSFORMATION

Jesus is our help and shield. No evil can destroy the soul that trusts in Christ even when, for a time, searing pain must riddle our path. "Our soul waits for the LORD; he is our help and our shield" (Psalm 33:20).

Christ understands suffering. He endured the darkest of all evil. He gave up His life on the cross. Satan could not destroy Him. And the grave could not hold Him. Christ rose to life and gives life, freedom, and joy to all who trust in Him.

All for good.
Believe and live.

(NOTE: If you're being or have been abused sexually, emotionally, verbally, or spiritually, seek professional help immediately. Abuse is sin, and God hates it.)

**What God permits, He works for good.
All else He restrains.**

Consider the truths in today's reading and write a response to the following question.

> *If I truly believe and act on what God has revealed in this passage, how will the motivations and attitudes of my heart transform and my actions be different tomorrow?*

_____

_____

Pray and confess any areas of unbelief today's reading revealed. Ask God to open your eyes to understanding and believing His Word, and for Him to empower you by His Spirit to obey and walk in the truth.

MEMORY VERSE

*Write out last week's and this week's memory verses
(Habakkuk 2:14, 1:5).*

Group Study Questions

WAITING ON GOD: HABAKKUK 1:1–11

• What stood out most to you from this week's lessons? How did it impact you?

• In what way(s) does God's name Yahweh comfort you?

• How does knowing that even the devil is God's devil change your perspective of headline news?

• It can be a fine line between biblical lament and whining or whimpering. Discuss ways we can determine if we've crossed the line.

• How has this week's lessons impacted your "O Lord, how long?" prayers?

- How might God be using a current trial you're enduring to bless you?

- Name one strategy you're now taking to ensure you wrestle with only God's plans, not His character.

- What are some of our most common tendencies that fuel our doubts? What are the truths that defeat these doubts?

- Which attribute of Christ most encouraged you this week?

BREAK UP INTO GROUPS OF TWO OR THREE.

Practice your memory verse with each other, share prayer requests, and then pray for each other.

> Look among the nations, and see;
>   wonder and be astounded.
> For I am doing a work in your days
>   that you would not believe if told.

—HABAKKUK 1:5

holding on
to Truth

HABAKKUK 1:12–17

TODAY'S READING

Habakkuk 1:12

INTENT

- Habakkuk has switched speakers again. The prophet is now addressing God.

TRUTH

On Saturday, January 13, 2018, at 8:07 a.m., a text message alert blared throughout the North Shore coffee shop on Oahu where my daughter Brittany worked. Everyone grabbed their cell phones and read the Hawaii Emergency Alert System message:

BALLISTIC THREAT INBOUND TO HAWAII.
SEEK IMMEDIATE SHELTER.
THIS IS NOT A DRILL.

Everyone in the coffee shop scattered to gather their loved ones and seek shelter.

My daughter jumped into her truck and sped off to find her boyfriend.

She called us from her truck to say goodbye.

Life seemed to flood from my body as panic shot through my bones.

This was one of those marker moments—a Matthew 16:15 moment, when Jesus asked, "Who do you say that I am?"

I steeled my heart.

"You are the Christ, the Son of the living God. I will trust in you."

Anchor Yourself in Christ

Trusting Christ doesn't ensure freedom from pain or sorrow, but when we anchor ourselves in Christ—ruler over all—the truth steels our confidence and helps quiet our fears.

While my husband talked with our daughter, I wondered, would this be the last time I'd hear her voice? My heart ached to hold her and keep her safe. But all I could do was entrust her to Christ's faithful and sovereign care.

Thirty-eight minutes and thirteen seconds after the Hawaiian authorities texted the doomsday alert, they admitted they sent it by mistake.

Relief—and understandable anger—flooded across Hawaii as families lifted their children out of sewers where they'd hidden them. My daughter and her boyfriend held each other with profound relief. Over four thousand miles away, Larry and I held each other and offered praise to the God who is not constrained by distance or world powers—or human error.

Habakkuk braced himself for a literal attack. He lifted his eyes to the Lord and anchored himself in God's unchanging character and promises.

Habakkuk 1:12 is so rich we'll cover only half of it today. We glanced at this verse in week 1, day 3.

Pray and study Habakkuk 1:12 in the chart. Note words or phrases that reveal the character, nature, and ways of God and that of anyone or anything else in the passage.

TRUTHS ABOUT GOD	VERSE	TRUTHS ABOUT OTHERS
	[12] Are you not from everlasting, O LORD my God, my Holy One? We shall not die. O LORD, you have ordained them as a judgment, and you, O Rock, have established them for reproof.	

God Is Everlasting

If a doctor has ever checked your reflexes by tapping below your knee, you've experienced a knee-jerk reaction. Habakkuk experienced an emotional knee-jerk reaction to God's announcement of Babylon—it was to remember truth. "Are you not from everlasting?" His rhetorical question affirmed that no matter what his heart wrestled with, he knew this to be true—God is the eternal one.

Since eternity past, God has established—and is faithful to—His character, Word, purposes, and plans. He can never change or else He'd cease to be God. But God can't cease to be God. If He could cease, He couldn't be God. You see where this is going, right?

God can never be untrue to His character, nature, or ways.

If we are faithless, he remains faithful—for he cannot deny himself. (2 Timothy 2:13)

List two ways this verse comforts you in our ever-changing times.

_____

_____

_____

Don't Worry about the Facts

God promised Abraham a son (Genesis 15). Twenty-five years later, still no child. (Our eternal God is never in a hurry.) Abraham, now one hundred years old, didn't worry about the *fact* that he was too old to father a son. Or the fact that Sarah's womb was as good as dead (Romans 4:19).

Abraham based his faith on who God is, not on science, as irrefutable as it seemed. God's promises are more irrefutable. Abraham's faith grew stronger, not weaker (v. 20). He and Sarah would have a son—regardless of the facts.

List some facts that fail in the face of God's promises. I'll start:

- Dead people can't live again, especially after four days in the grave. Except they can when Christ says they can. "Lazarus, come out." See John 11.

_____

_____

_____

_____

Yahweh Holds Us Fast

Not only will Yahweh never cast out those who belong to Him, even better, He holds us secure. No one can snatch us out of His hand (John 10:28). We can't fall, roll, or leap out either. Christ holds on to us. Not the other way around.

Habakkuk understood that Judah's survival as a covenant nation didn't depend on their character but on God's. "We shall not die" (Habakkuk 1:12).

If you're a Christian, how secure do you feel about your salvation? Do you understand your eternal security depends on Yahweh's ability to hold you forever, not on your ability to hold on to your salvation?

Read John 10:28–29; Philippians 1:6; 2 Thessalonians 3:3; and Jude 24.

Elohim Doesn't Need Us—but He Wants Us

After Habakkuk focused on the love of God, he reminded himself of the supremacy of God. "O LORD my God," or literally "O Yahweh my Elohim." My supreme and sovereign God—the all-sufficient and uncreated Creator. Nothing exists outside His control. He has no needs.

Elohim didn't create us or the heavenly hosts because He was lonely or had a need. The Father, Son, and Holy Spirit are fully satisfied within their relationship—within the Trinity. Heaven is perfect without us. And yet He created us.

If you belong to Christ, let this marvelous truth soak in: **the Lord God (Yahweh Elohim) doesn't need you—but He wants you.**

Circle the words below that express why God created us.

Everyone who is called by my name,
    whom I created for my glory,
    whom I formed and made.
        —Isaiah 43:7

What would it say about God if He *needed* us?

_____

_____

The Lord God Is the Holy One

The Hebrew word for *holy* is *qādôš*.[9] It means to be set apart, completely different from the ordinary, the common.

God's holiness transcends all. He's set apart and utterly different from all creation. God doesn't make himself holy. He is holy.

- God's holiness adorns all His other attributes.
- His love is holy, set apart from even the hint of selfishness.
- His wisdom is holy, set apart from all foolishness or guesswork.
- His justice is holy, set apart from even the suggestion of injustice.

We can't fully understand God, but no one can question Him any more than a toddler can question a rocket scientist about his designs.

Our everlasting God has all knowledge from eternity to eternity. He established His plans and purposes out of His holy wisdom, love, and justice, and all His other traits. No one is better able to judge what is good and right to do—and to allow humankind to do—than the holy Judge of all. Even if His plan is to send an evil nation to bring violence upon a people more righteous than them.

How does understanding God's holiness help you face the troubles in the world, your life, and the lives of your loved ones?

_____

_____

TRANSFORMATION

Jesus is holy (Mark 1:24; Acts 4:27; Hebrews 7:26). Christ took the form of common man, but there's nothing common about Him. Jesus, the Holy One, is with you always.

We all have assumptions and knee-jerk reactions. Sleeping babies elicit smiles. Nuclear missiles prompt terror. But day by day, Christ is teaching us to anchor our knee-jerk reactions on Him—the Holy One of God.

Which of the following most accurately reflects your current knee-jerk reaction when trouble crashes in?

- Panic. Laser-focused on the problem, not God.
- Anger. "You're unfair, God! How could you let this happen?"
- Despair. "Why do you hate me, God?"
- Fretting. "Please, oh please, oh please!"
- Truth: "You are from everlasting, O Lord my God, my Holy One."

Are you like me? Can you check each depending on the day? Growing in Christlikeness is a journey. Fortunately, God promised to do the work in us (Philippians 1:6; 2:13).

Christis our best knee-jerk reaction.

Consider the truths in today's reading and write a response to the following questions.

If I truly believe and act on what God has revealed in this passage, how will I be changed? How will the motivations and attitudes of my heart transform and my actions be different tomorrow?

Pray and confess any areas of unbelief today's reading revealed. Ask God to open your eyes to understanding and believing His Word, and for Him to empower you by His Spirit to obey and walk in the truth.

MEMORY VERSE

Recite this week's memory verse aloud five times:

Are you not from everlasting,
　　O LORD my God, my Holy One?
　　We shall not die.
O LORD, you have ordained them as a judgment,
　　and you, O Rock, have established them for reproof.

—HABAKKUK 1:12

TODAY'S READING

Habakkuk 1:12

INTENT

- God made two types of covenants with Israel— unconditional and conditional.
- Abrahamic covenant—God's unconditional promise to be Israel's God, bless the world through Abraham (Messiah would come through his line), and to give Israel the land of Canaan as an "everlasting possession" (Genesis 17:8).
- Mosaic covenant—God's conditional promise that if Israel obeyed God's law, they'd be blessed. If they refused, they'd suffer consequences, which included foreign powers overthrowing them and removing them from their land for a time (Deuteronomy 28).

TRUTH

Jesus said to His disciples, "Let not your hearts be troubled" (John 14:1).

He said this after He'd told them that one of them would betray Him, He would soon leave them, and Peter would deny he even knew Jesus that very evening.

How could their hearts not be troubled?

This is how: by believing God's Word when He said, "Believe in God; believe also in me" (v. 1).

Today we'll look at the second half of our verse. Pray and study Habakkuk 1:12 in the chart. Note words or phrases that reveal the character, nature, and ways of God and that of anyone or anything else in the passage.

TRUTHS ABOUT GOD	VERSE	TRUTHS ABOUT OTHERS
	[12] Are you not from everlasting, O LORD my God, my Holy One? We shall not die. O LORD, you have ordained them as a judgment, and you, O Rock, have established them for reproof.	

Babylons Cannot Void God's Promises

God was raising up a "fearsome" nation to swoop down on Judah (Habakkuk 1:7–8). The Hebrew term Habakkuk used for *fearsome* can also describe "the terror instilled by the bared teeth of a crocodile."[10] It hardly sounds like Judah would get out alive. But Habakkuk wasn't delusional when he said, "We shall not die." He'd anchored himself in God and His promises. He made his conclusions in the context of God's character and covenants, not Babylon's fearsomeness.

• God is the eternal, unchanging Yahweh, the covenant-keeping God, supreme and sovereign over all the earth. He's holy in all He is and does.

• God promised Abraham that He'd give them Canaan as an everlasting possession. Even if He chose to loan it to Babylon for a time, eventually they'd return to the land.

• God promised Messiah would come through Judah. They might have to serve under Babylon for a time, but Judah would not perish.

• Babylon would not—could not—void God's promises. The nation of the Jews would not end (Jeremiah 31:35–36; 33:23–26).

Each of us has our own Babylon—circumstances or people God places into our lives to discipline or refine us. Despite anyone's threats, no one can void a single promise of God. And one of the promises Jesus gave us is, "In the world you will have tribulation" (John 16:33). This isn't an exciting promise, but it's sandwiched between two glorious promises: "I have said these things to you, that in me you may have peace" and "But take heart; I have overcome the world." Peace and power belong to us in Christ.

Many other promises confirm that God works everything that touches our lives for our good and His glory. Why should we worry? His promises never fail, including the one that He'll make us like Christ (Romans 8:29). But sometimes that means He'll take us to hard places to fulfill this promise.

God Leads Us into Hard Places

Habakkuk didn't stumble over the truth *that* God ordains and establishes everything, even Babylons. Instead, he stumbled over *what* God had ordained and established.

But doesn't it make God sound mean if we say He *ordains* and *establishes* Babylons? If God ordained our hard places simply to crush us, we might have an argument. But God's purposes are to purify His bride. To expose and rid us of the sin that seeks to destroy us. God knows the right time and way to purify us—like when He rescued Israel out of slavery in Egypt and then led them into the barren wilderness.

God intentionally led Israel into the wilderness to a place without drinkable water. Israel accused God of bringing them out of Egypt to kill them.

But just as God had planned, He turned their bitter water sweet and then led them to twelve fresh springs (Exodus 15:22–27).

Around the next boulder, God led them to hunger.

Again, Israel accused Him of nefarious intentions.

But just as God had planned, He sent quail in the evening and bread from heaven in the morning (16:1–21).

Deeper into the barren wilderness, God led them to a place with no water at all—fresh or bitter.

Again, Israel said, "God is trying to kill us."

Just as He'd planned, God commanded Moses to take his staff (the symbol of God's power) and strike the rock at Horeb. When Moses struck the rock, rivers of water flowed out. Enough water for all the people. From a rock (17:1–7).

Four times, God exposed Israel's unbelief—their knee-jerk reaction to every trial. Four times, God proved His promises are true and His power is unmatched.

Are we like the Israelites? Are we too focused on the bitterness of our trials to believe in and taste God's goodness?

> Consider your current trial. What might God be teaching you about himself? List some truths about Him that will help you taste His goodness rather than the bitterness of your trial.

_____

_____

_____

_____

_____

> To go deeper, read Numbers 13:17–14:4 and Deuteronomy 32:1–47, and consider then write what it tells us about our God and Israel's heart (which reflects ours).

_____

_____

In the wilderness, God promised to bless Israel, but they whined for forty years—while Moses, Joshua, and Caleb worshipped.

In Judah, God declared judgment against them using a nation as fearsome as the bared teeth of a crocodile—and still Habakkuk worshipped.

Trials expose our true faith, whether it's built on sinking sand or on the Rock.

TRANSFORMATION

Jesus is the Rock. God struck Christ for our sins so that rivers of living water would pour into His children and give us eternal life and the power to walk in the truth. Christ preserved Israel in the wilderness, and He will preserve His church. We will not die.

"And all drank the same spiritual drink. For they drank from the spiritual Rock that followed them, and the Rock was Christ" (1 Corinthians 10:4).

On the third day after Jesus died, the disciples discovered what God has been proving from the beginning. His promises never fail. Jesus rose from the dead, just as He said He would.

"Let not your hearts be troubled. Believe in God; believe also in me" (John 14:1).

My hope is built on nothing less
Than Jesus' blood and righteousness.
I dare not trust the sweetest frame,
But wholly lean on Jesus' name.
On Christ the solid rock I stand,
All other ground is sinking sand.
　　—Edward Mote, "My Hope Is Built" (1834)

Trials expose our true faith, whether it's built on sinking sand or on the Rock.

Consider the truths in today's reading and write a response to the following question.

> *If I truly believe and act on what God has revealed in this passage, how will the motivations and attitudes of my heart transform and my actions be different tomorrow?*

_____

_____

Pray and confess any areas of unbelief today's reading revealed. Ask God to open your eyes to understanding and believing His Word, and for Him to empower you by His Spirit to obey and walk in the truth.

MEMORY VERSE

Write out this week's memory verse: Habakkuk 1:12.

TODAY'S READING

Habakkuk 1:13

INTENT

- In this verse, Habakkuk's question is sincere, not rhetorical.

TRUTH

Stop me if you've heard this story.

A local church held a luncheon. The sign on the basket of apples read, "Take only one. God is watching." Farther down the food table sat the desserts. Its sign read, "Take all you want. God is watching the apples."

Our all-seeing God is not so busy watching the apples that He doesn't notice the Babylons of our world or care about their evil. He knows every thought, word, and deed of every person, creature, and heavenly power. He sees all evil and hates it. He is of "purer eyes" (Habakkuk 1:13). His holiness prevents Him from looking at the wicked and wrong with favor.

Pray and study Habakkuk 1:13 in the chart. Note words or phrases that reveal the character, nature, and ways of God and that of anyone or anything else in the passage.

TRUTHS ABOUT GOD	VERSE	TRUTHS ABOUT OTHERS
	[13] You who are of purer eyes than to see evil and cannot look at wrong, why do you idly look at traitors and remain silent when the wicked swallows up the man more righteous than he?	

All We Need to Know

Fear and confusion gripped Habakkuk. He couldn't understand how a holy God could enlist the services of a nation more evil than Judah to swallow them up. How could the Holy One remain silent in the days when Babylon would rage in violence against Judah?

Don't we watch the news and struggle with the same question?

We want to trust God, but there's so much we don't understand. So much that seems to go against everything we know about Him.

While we *want* to know every detail about what concerns us, we say we *need* to know.

Why do we think we need to know?

I need to know if all my loved ones will be saved because how can I be happy if I don't know?

I need to know I'll have enough money to live each day because how can I not fear the future if I don't know?

I need to know! Tell me, God.

God understands our desire to know, but when we say we *need* to know, we've stepped out of innocent curiosity and into prideful demanding.

Our faith is resting in our desired outcome, not in Christ.

When our faith rests securely in Him, our perceived needs melt away—or almost away. We're human after all—like Habakkuk.

The answers to all our fears and confusions about God, His ways, and this world are answered in His Word. He doesn't owe us any further explanation than He's already given us. His Word is sufficient.

Do you truly believe that God's Word contains all we actually need to know right now?

On a scale of 1 to 10, with 1 being "I need to know everything" and 10 being "I'm in perfect peace with waiting on God," where does your current need to know fall on the scale?

I NEED TO KNOW EVERYTHING		I'M IN PERFECT PEACE WITH WAITING ON GOD
0	5	10

I've been at level 10. I think. For a second. Maybe.

We're on a lifelong journey of God moving us from "tell me now" to "I trust you." Keep walking.

Walk by Faith, Not by Sight

Every believer in history has had to walk by faith, not by sight. None of us know the whole story of God's eternal plans and purposes—the red thread of Jesus woven from Genesis through Revelation. He's revealed much, but we see it all as if looking through a dim reflection in a blurred mirror (1 Corinthians 13:12). He didn't reveal every detail of His plans even to His prophets.

Read Deuteronomy 29:29 and 1 Peter 1:10–12.

Did the prophets know that when God led Israel out of slavery in Egypt through the Red Sea, it pointed to Christ leading us out of slavery to sin and into new life in Him?

Did they know the bronze serpent Moses lifted up in the wilderness symbolized Christ being lifted up on the cross for our sins (John 3:14–15)?

God used these and many other events—including Babylon—to create a road map to Jesus, the promised Savior. But God's prophets and people couldn't understand it all. We understand more because we have more revealed history to look back on (namely the cross), but there's still much we don't understand. We can and must trust God with what we don't know.

The Struggle with God's Sovereignty

God is either sovereign over all, or He cannot be sovereign at all.

God's sovereignty means that
He does whatever He wants
with whoever He wants
whenever He wants
for whatever purposes He wants.

This explanation of God's sovereignty used to scare me. But then I learned that everything God desires and does is good and pure. His ways are always holy and loving toward His children. Thus, God's sovereignty means we're going to be okay.

Habakkuk knew and agreed with this truth. But he also knew Judah was rife with sin, and because God is holy, He must judge their sin. He'd been praying for God to revive them and even discipline them. But with Babylon? With someone more sinful than Judah?

The Babylon dilemma caused Habakkuk to struggle with God's sovereignty like my friend who told me she's not afraid of dying but of how much it might hurt. Habakkuk knew he could trust God's ways, but he feared the pain and sorrow that His ways would bring Judah.

No matter how much a situation grieves or confuses us, we can rest in God. He's sovereign even over our pain and sorrow.

Does God's sovereignty scare you? If so, write down three of God's unfailing character traits and apply them to His sovereignty. For instance, since God is love, His sovereign choices in our life must rise out of His love for us.

_____

_____

_____

If we knew everything God knows, we'd do everything God does exactly how He does it.

We Default to Our Training

At a safety seminar, the instructor taught that we default to our training in a crisis. If a shooter enters a room, we'll karate chop the gunman *if* we've been thoroughly trained. Otherwise, we'll likely freeze or panic.

He taught that our best chance of survival in such an instance is to form the habit now of locating every exit whenever we enter a room. Then, if the worst happens, our default training will kick in. We'll already know the best exit for escape and have a better chance to lead others to safety. No karate needed.

For years I've been training myself to recall God's character, nature, and ways. Now, whenever I get upset or frustrated, my default training kicks in. A list of what I know to be true about God pops into my mind.

I'm still learning to believe these truths, but at least I have a good list to choose from to help build my faith. Truths such as God is sovereign, good, and holy in all His ways. He cannot do evil. He's just and merciful. His love and grace abound. His wisdom is unfailing. He sees the end from the beginning and causes all things to conspire together for the good of His children.

I can trust Him but not my ability to properly understand or interpret everything I see. Every day God is teaching me to submit my emotions to the truth I know (2 Corinthians 10:5).

Commit to daily reminding yourself of God's attributes.

Start by writing keywords or phrases from the following verses on God's sovereignty.

Ephesians 1:11

Romans 8:28

Proverbs 16:33

Job 42:2

Lamentations 3:37–39

Acts 4:27–28

TRANSFORMATION

Jesus is the visible image of our invisible God (Colossians 1:15). To see Christ is to see the Father and His tender love. The four Gospels overflow with rich displays of Christ's glorious attributes. May these truths overwhelm your fears and instill you with confidence in our almighty God and our Lord and Savior.

No scheme of Satan or enemy plot could succeed in keeping Christ from His glorious purpose—the salvation of all who believe in Him. This same Jesus oversees the affairs of our lives—the apples and desserts, the Babylons and gunmen, and the needs of every hurting heart.

If we knew everything God knows, we'd do everything God does exactly how He does it.

Consider the truths in today's reading and write a response to the following question.

If I truly believe and act on what God has revealed in this passage, how will the motivations and attitudes of my heart transform and my actions be different tomorrow?

Pray and confess any areas of unbelief today's reading revealed. Ask God to open your eyes to understanding and believing His Word, and for Him to empower you by His Spirit to obey and walk in the truth.

MEMORY VERSE

Write out this week's memory verse: Habakkuk 1:12.

TODAY'S READING

Habakkuk 1:14–16

INTENT

- Fishing was a major industry in Babylon.
- Artwork found on ancient Near Eastern walls shows conquering rulers and deities dragging prisoners off in nets like fish.

TRUTH

God made us to worship. My friend Marshall worshipped revenge and rage.

Blood and bruises marked Marshall's childhood as his parents worshipped at the altars of alcohol and violence. Many nights Marshall hid in his bedroom, hoping they wouldn't burst through his door and beat him.

When he was old enough, he sought safety in the army. They shipped him to Vietnam. In the thick jungles of Nam, he once again spent nights hiding from his enemy, just trying to survive.

Marshall returned an angry and dangerous man. Bowing to his parents' altars of alcohol and rage, he added drugs to his menagerie of idols. His obsessions hooked him like a fish in the sea . . . and landed him in prison. Scarred by the sins of others and twisted by the sins he worshipped, Marshall hit rock bottom.

We All Worship

It's not a matter of *if* we worship but *what* we worship.

Babylon worshipped their strength, success, and the treasures they plundered from those they crushed. They made sacrifices and offerings to the tools of their trade as if these cruel instruments had divinely decreed their success.

They drove fishhooks through the lower lips of their prisoners and marched them to Babylon by ropes strung through the eyehooks. They treated their captives "like the fish of the sea, like crawling things that have no ruler" (Habakkuk 1:14).

Perverse joy fueled them as they celebrated the suffering they inflicted.

God made us to worship. What we worship makes us.

Pray and study Habakkuk 1:14–16 in the chart. Note words or phrases that reveal the character, nature, and ways of God and that of anyone or anything else in the passage.

TRUTHS ABOUT GOD	VERSE	TRUTHS ABOUT OTHERS
	¹⁴ You make mankind like the fish of the sea, like crawling things that have no ruler.	
	¹⁵ He brings all of them up with a hook; he drags them out with his net; he gathers them in his dragnet; so he rejoices and is glad.	
	¹⁶ Therefore he sacrifices to his net and makes offerings to his dragnet; for by them he lives in luxury, and his food is rich.	

There's No End to What We'll Worship

Apart from Christ's power at work in us, we'll all bow to sin and descend as far as it will take us—and sin is never satisfied. It will twist truth and distort our thoughts until it consumes us.

Satan dresses up sin and disguises it as delightful and delicious. And harmless. All the while sin's hooks sink into us and lead us where it wants us to go.

It promises to make our dreams come true. We didn't know the dream was a nightmare.

Unless the Lord intervenes, humankind will move from *recoiling* to *worshipping* the most heinous of crimes. A sin one generation detests, the next generations will tolerate, then accept, and then finally worship. And like the religious leaders in Jesus's day, they'll do it in the name of "love," "rights," and "the greater good."

I bet you're ready for some hope now.

Read Romans 5:20–21 below.

Where sin increased, grace abounded all the more, so that, as sin reigned in death, grace also might reign through righteousness leading to eternal life through Jesus Christ our Lord.

Scratch out the phrases about sin and death. What remains reveals the hope and confidence that empowers us to walk in a world filled with Judahs and Babylons—and us. Jesus has defeated sin and death. One day, He'll destroy them forever.

But what about now? Must we wait for heaven to live in abiding joy?

Keep reading. Joy today is around the corner.

God Made Jesus Low to Raise Us Up

For most of Jesus's ministry, He was the most popular man in Israel. Crowds followed Him everywhere, especially after He borrowed a young boy's lunch and fed over five thousand people. His fame skyrocketed after He raised Lazarus from the dead. Lazarus had been in the grave four days when Jesus called him out.

In Jerusalem, though, the very ones who should have led Israel to worship Christ gathered to discuss the *problem* He'd become.

Read John 11:45–53.

What problem did the leaders say they had with Jesus (v. 48)? (This reveals what they worshipped.)

_____

What did the leaders decide to do with Jesus (v. 53)? (This reveals how far sin will take us.)

_____

What/who ordained their decision (v. 51)? (This displays the truth Habakkuk embraced although it perplexed him.)

_____

Why was it necessary for God to work through the most insidious crime in history—crucifying the Son of God? (See 1 Peter 3:18.)

_____

_____

God made Jesus "for a little while . . . lower than the angels" so His enemies could lift Him up on the cruel cross for the sin of the world (Hebrews 2:9). God's wisdom is perfect and infinite. He would never have sent His own Son to the cross if there were any other way to purchase our freedom from sin. Jesus made this clear as He prayed in the garden of Gethsemane.

Write out Jesus's prayer in Matthew 26:39.

_____

_____

We see at least three truths in this verse that offer comfort:

1. Jesus lamented the suffering sin brings. He fell on His face as He lamented.
2. Jesus confirmed God's will is best, even when it brings temporary suffering.
3. God made Jesus low to raise us up. Jesus endured death so He could raise worshippers of God to eternal life and make us sons and daughters.

God Does No Wrong

God's sovereign power rules over the heavens and the earth. Whatever He declares is as good as done (Romans 4:17).

This truth both comforted and troubled Habakkuk.

It comforted him because no evil can touch us if God says no. He's our strong tower.

It troubled Habakkuk because God doesn't always say no. Sometimes in His wisdom He says yes. (Ask Job.)

God never pushed Judah into worshipping idols and other evil, but neither did He step in and stop them. And now, He called forth an extreme instrument of discipline, of destruction.

The shock led Habakkuk to almost charge God with wrong in Habakkuk 1:14, as if God had trapped Judah in a fishbowl and invited the army of Babylon to fish in it with nets.

Habakkuk wasn't wrong about God's sovereign power. His heart simply needed directing. God had indeed brought Judah low, but He had done Judah no wrong.

Do you ever feel like God has done you wrong? List any areas of your life which Satan could use to tempt you to believe this lie.

Perhaps you're suffering from a chronic medical condition. Or an addiction. Or you've lost your job.

_____

_____

_____

_____

Examine your heart. If Satan were to tempt you to worship someone or something other than God, what would he dangle before your eyes?

_____

_____

Sin brought my friend Marshall low, but God lifted him out of his sin and poured healing rivers of living water into his soul through Christ. He brought Marshall's spiritually dead heart to life and turned a dangerous man filled with hate into a pastor filled with abiding joy, peace, and love.

When actress Jeannette Clift George prepared to portray World War II concentration camp survivor Corrie ten Boom in the movie *The Hiding Place*, the characteristic that most impressed her was Corrie's joy.

Elisabeth Elliot wrote of Corrie's joy, "Now where did that come from? Was it because everything in her life worked so beautifully? Was it because she had had a happy life as the world would define happiness? Of course not. Her perspective was transfigured. And she, herself, was transfigured for the benefit of the rest of us. We were given a visible sign in the face of Corrie Ten Boom of an invisible reality."[11]

What we see in Corrie—and Habakkuk and Marshall—is the abiding joy that comes from worshipping Christ.

TRANSFORMATION

Jesus is worthy. "Worthy is the Lamb who was slain, to receive power and wealth and wisdom and might and honor and glory and blessing!" (Revelation 5:12).

Babylon worshipped their gods, their nets, and themselves—and suffered the consequences. But Jesus is worthy of all our worship and praise. God brings us low so we can see the truth. Worshipping Christ works a miracle in our hearts that covers our sorrows with joy that does not fade because He is worthy.

We don't all experience trauma to the level Corrie or Marshall endured—the kind that leaves emotional and physical scars—but we all suffer. What we suffer doesn't determine what we become. What we worship does.

God made us to worship. What we worship makes us.

Worship the Lamb who is worthy. Worship Christ.

TRANSFORMATIONAL TRUTH

God made us to worship.
What we worship makes us.

Consider the truths in today's reading and write a response to the following question.

If I truly believe and act on what God has revealed in this passage, how will the motivations and attitudes of my heart transform and my actions be different tomorrow?

Pray and confess any areas of unbelief today's reading revealed. Ask God to open your eyes to understanding and believing His Word, and for Him to empower you by His Spirit to obey and walk in the truth.

Write out this week's memory verse: Habakkuk 1:12.

TODAY'S READING

Habakkuk 1:17

INTENT

• Habakkuk used the symbolism of a fishing net to describe how Nebuchadnezzar dragged prisoners like fish to Babylon, emptied his metaphorical nets, and set out to conquer more nations. His lust for power and control seemed endless.

TRUTH

When Vera told me she survived the killing fields of Cambodia, I could barely breathe. I looked into her gentle eyes and marveled. How could this tiny lady have survived the violent genocide of over a million people at the hands of the ruthless dictator Pol Pot and his evil regime? Her husband didn't.

How often did Vera pray as she sheltered their baby, "Will Pol Pot keep on mercilessly killing forever?"

As Vera told me of the horrors she suffered, across town Lucy was surviving a different war. Each morning she awakened and wondered what her day would bring married to a man ruled by anger.

As I prayed for her, I wondered why God didn't stop him. Is God going to let her husband keep on mercilessly hurting her forever?

God's answer for both was the same.

No.

Pray and study Habakkuk 1:17 in the chart. Note words or phrases that reveal the character, nature, and ways of God and that of anyone or anything else in the passage.

TRUTHS ABOUT GOD	VERSE	TRUTHS ABOUT OTHERS
	[17] Is he then to keep on emptying his net and mercilessly killing nations forever?	

The End from the Beginning

Our world wasn't evil in the beginning, but it got there fast. In a moment of time, the deed was done. Satan tempted, and Adam and Eve sinned.

Had God watched Satan play out his wicked scheme and hoped Adam and Eve would stand strong? Did He scramble to craft a plan to get them out of their mess? Or had He abandoned them in anger over their sin?

No. No. And no.

God is not like us. God doesn't just see the end from the beginning. He declared it.

Read Isaiah 46:9–11.

God wove the red thread of Jesus into history long before He created Satan and Adam and Eve. The promise of salvation in Genesis 3:15, the crucifixion of God's Son in Mark 15:24, and Satan's destruction in Revelation 20:10 were already written.

How does realizing each of these moments were ordained before the foundation of the earth make you feel? Journal your thoughts.

_____

_____

_____

_____

God's Sovereignty and Man's Free Will

Out of the evil in their own hearts, the Babylonians marched toward Judah. They set their faces forward, oblivious that they were fulfilling God's purpose for them and the words spoken about them by at least five prophets.

Whatever your day brings, it's not a rogue event. It's part of the ordained tapestry of God's plan to bring all things under Christ's righteous rule. But this doesn't mean we're helpless puppets tied to our master's strings. We freely choose, and these choices impact us and those around us. But the fate of the world doesn't hinge on us. It rests in God and His sovereignty.

How God works His sovereignty through man's free will is a deep and mysterious truth overseen by the all-wise and holy Yahweh Elohim.

We can rest in His mystery even if we can't fully understand it.

It All Begins and Ends with Christ

Every event in history and every breath we breathe is from, through, and to Christ (Romans 11:36). It's all about Him. He's the point of the Bible and of life.

As humans, we'll struggle to accept that our lives are about Christ's glory, not ours and our accomplishments. But as Christians, this should thrill us—especially as we think about Christ's story.

The infant Jesus was placed in an animal food trough then rushed off to Egypt to escape an earthly king's murderous rampage.

The Holy Spirit led Jesus into the wilderness to be tempted by Satan for forty grueling days.

His friend Judas betrayed Him to men who should've led the world to worship Him, not arrest Him.

Soldiers spit on Christ, beat Him until He was almost unrecognizable.

They thrust a crown of thorns onto His head and drove nails through His hands and feet.

They crucified our Lord.

For six hours, Jesus suffered on the cross as God laid on Him the sins of the world.

Jesus drank the full cup of God's wrath for our sin, proclaimed, "It is finished!" and died.

All by the sovereign will of God.

When I think of His story and what He endured for me—for you—I can barely breathe.

Ah, but then comes resurrection.

And glory.

And honor.

And pleasures forever.

Are You Suffering?

If you're suffering today, reflect on Christ's story.

Your pain and suffering will not last if you belong to Him. He purchased you for himself. He will not be denied His child. Evil will not continue to empty its nets and kill forever. Your resurrection is coming.

If you don't belong to Christ, this life may bring you all your heart desires. But then comes judgment. Not glory, honor, or pleasures forever.

Turn to Christ in faith today.

His is the story of resurrection glory for all who will believe. Believe today.

Happily Ever After

My friend Julie's son survived a serious car accident, but barely. He remained in a medically induced coma for days, teetering on the edge of death. Friends stopped by the hospital to comfort her and praised her for her testimony of faith. She told me through anguished tears, "I don't want to be a testimony. I just want my son."

I wonder if Habakkuk felt a little like Julie. *Lord, I don't want to be in this part of your grand story. I just want peace.*

Peace will come. The glories of Christ's eternal kingdom are always in view. Every Christian *will* live happily ever after.

But first, we have a role to play that He's designed for us.

God is taking the tattered threads of our lives and our world and creating a masterpiece to reflect the glories of Christ to the world. Some of it will hurt. Some of it may terrify us. But Christ works it together for the good of those who love Him, the blessing of many, and His great glory.

We can know this is all true in our heads but knowing it and embracing it aren't the same. Habakkuk encourages us with his example of embracing God's sovereign will. He leads us along this bumpy but faithful path that always leads to joy.

How might God be using the hard stories in your life to weave a masterpiece of faith in your heart for your good, the blessing of others, and His great glory?

_____

_____

_____

TRANSFORMATION

Jesus is the resurrection and the life (John 11:25). Whatever God calls us to endure, this is not the end. In Christ, we have risen to new life, and when He returns, we'll reign forever with Him.

I don't know the end of my story on earth. Or Vera's. Or Lucy's. Or yours. But I know Christ is creating a masterpiece out of the threads of our pain and sorrow that will be to His praise and glory and will make our joy complete.

Resurrection is coming.

And when God has fulfilled every word in the Bible, our story will read:

And they lived happily ever after.

Resurrection is coming. And they lived happily ever after.

Consider the truths in today's reading and write a response to the following question.

> *If I truly believe and act on what God has revealed in this passage, how will the motivations and attitudes of my heart transform and my actions be different tomorrow?*

_____

_____

Pray and confess any areas of unbelief today's reading revealed. Ask God to open your eyes to understanding and believing His Word, and for Him to empower you by His Spirit to obey and walk in the truth.

MEMORY VERSE

*Write out each memory verse we've learned so far
(Habakkuk 2:14; 1:5; 1:12).*

Group Study Questions

HOLDING ON TO TRUTH: HABAKKUK 1:12–17

- What stood out most to you from this week's lessons? How did it impact you?

- What tends to be your knee-jerk reaction to trouble?

- What in this week's lessons impacted your ability to see blessings in God's silence or in His not answering your prayers as you wanted?

- If Satan wanted to tempt you to worship someone or something other than God, what would he dangle before your eyes?

• Discuss this statement: If we knew everything God knows, we'd do everything God does exactly how He does it.

• How does the assurance of resurrection comfort you in your trials?

• Share a tip you use that's helped you memorize the truths in God's Word.

• Which attribute of Christ most encouraged you this week?

BREAK UP INTO GROUPS OF TWO OR THREE.

Practice your memory verse with each other, share prayer requests, and then pray for each other.

> Are you not from everlasting,
> O LORD my God, my Holy One?
> We shall not die.
> O LORD, you have ordained them as a judgment,
> and you, O Rock, have established them for reproof.

> **—HABAKKUK 1:12**

living
by faith

HABAKKUK 2:1-5

TODAY'S READING

Habakkuk 2:1

INTENT

• In ancient days, kings set watchmen on towers to scan the horizon for the enemy or a messenger bringing news.

• The ending of this verse varies depending on the translation, but the point is the same. Habakkuk will need to respond when God corrects his thinking.

TRUTH

Who's the guilty party in the case of the Leaning Tower of Pisa? The architect Pisano? Or Gerardo? The true architect remains a mystery. I'd probably want to hide my identity. After all, a bell tower is a simple project for a skilled architect, even without modern technology. Yet even before builders reached the fourth level, the tower tilted due to a soft foundation.

Pray and study Habakkuk 2:1 in the chart. Note words or phrases that reveal the character, nature, and ways of God and that of anyone or anything else in the passage.

TRUTHS ABOUT GOD	VERSE	TRUTHS ABOUT OTHERS
	[1] I will take my stand at my watch-post and station myself on the tower, and look out to see what he will say to me, and what I will answer concerning my complaint.	

Lean into Christ

After God declared to Habakkuk that He was sending Babylon, Habakkuk's faith wobbled, but it didn't fall. Fear, doubt, and confusion rose, but they couldn't topple his faith. It rested on the firm foundation of God's Word and character. Though anxiety's relentless trio caused his faith to lean, he knew how to right it. He leaned into Yahweh Elohim.

Habakkuk lifted his concerns and confusion (aka complaints) to the Lord, climbed the watchtower of his heart to seek God's wisdom and correction, and waited expectantly for Him to answer.

Two Questions for Your Troubled Heart

Over the years I've learned to ask my troubled heart two searching questions:

1. **Lord, what do I not know about you right now that I need to know?** Sometimes our hearts trouble us because we simply haven't learned a truth about God that would remove our fears. Study God's Word and His character.

2. **Lord, what do I not believe about you right now that I need to believe?** We all have areas and moments of unbelief. God mercifully uses our circumstances to expose them. We want to know we have a hole in our boat before we head into deep waters.

At some point, every person's life ventures into deep waters.

Seek and Embrace God's Wisdom

Habakkuk wanted to understand. He knew God alone possesses perfect wisdom. Human wisdom is often pure foolishness (Adam and Eve's wisdom told them to believe a talking serpent over God— Genesis 3).

Instead of outlining how we feel God should answer our prayers, let's seek His wisdom.

Read 2 Chronicles 20:1–12. List the steps Jehoshaphat followed when trouble crashed in.

_____

In what ways does Jehoshaphat's prayer reflect Habakkuk's?

_____

_____

Jehoshaphat's remembrances of God filled six verses. His request filled one. He anchored himself in the bedrock of God Almighty without downplaying the seriousness of his predicament.

Write out 2 Chronicles 20:12 and pray Jehoshaphat's prayer concerning your deepest concerns.

_____

_____

_____

_____

Seek and Embrace God's Correction

Even when we're sincere in seeking the right course of action, we can be sincerely wrong. We need God's correction when we stray. Jehoshaphat strayed. He lost his position as our role model in a few short verses. Are we less susceptible to poor judgment than godly Jehoshaphat?

Read 2 Chronicles 20:35–37.

Jehoshaphat thought it would be fine to team up with a wicked king. What could go wrong? Whenever God exposes our unbelief, mistaken understandings, confusion, or sin, let's embrace His correction with humble hearts. Prideful hearts push back, ignore God's conviction, or curl up in despair.

When we desire God's glory above all, we embrace His wise leading. Even if His plans hurt, we can trust Him.

God only brings faithful pain, never wasted sorrow.

Write out Psalm 139:23–24.

_____

_____

_____

_____

Examine your heart. Does it lean toward humility or pride? Be honest with yourself. God gives grace to the humble.

_____

_____

Write out the verses below.

Psalm 51:17

_____

_____

_____

Matthew 23:12

_____

_____

_____

Wait Expectantly

Habakkuk stationed himself on his watchpost and waited expectantly for God to answer. The humble heart rests in the holy and good God who writes history in advance.

How often do we wait on the Lord like a child who jumps up and down and claps because she knows her father will keep his promise? Or do we repeat fretful prayers as if God might not hear us or has to be convinced to do us good?

Do we offer God advice as if He needs our counsel and then slump off, dragging our fears and confusion behind us? Or do we pray about our deepest concerns and stand up eager to trust His answer, even if it's the opposite of what we prayed?

Years ago, I developed the habit of laying all my concerns before God in the morning often with tears and then praising Him for who He is the rest of the day. Not, "I praise you that you can fix this problem," but rather, "I praise you because your ways are always good and right."

Even in the context of praise, focusing on our problems causes our emotions to tilt our faith. Focusing on God alone builds strong, not tottering, faith.

Consider the following illustration. If you desperately needed a job, which prayer would best reflect Habakkuk's approach?

• Father, please, please, please give me a good-paying job. I'll lose my home and my car if you don't. Please, oh, please God. I know you can. I don't know what I'll do if you don't. I'm desperate. I need to know you hear me. Amen.

• O Lord God, you are the Holy One. You created the heavens and the earth, and you rule it all. There's nothing you don't own. Father, I need a job, and I don't have the money to pay my rent or car loan. I don't know what to do, but my eyes are on you, my Rock and my Provider. You bring water from a rock and send bread from heaven. I look to you to meet my needs according to your kind purposes. Glorify yourself in me as I wait on you. Amen.

What emotions did you feel as you read each prayer? Why do you think these prayers evoked these emotions?

_____

_____

_____

_____

Which prayer most reflects your current prayer life when trouble crashes in?

_____

Write out Psalm 123:2.

_____

_____

_____

_____

_____

Write out Jeremiah 32:17.

_____

_____

_____

_____

_____

TRANSFORMATION

Jesus is the architect, builder, and never-failing foundation of our faith (1 Corinthians 3:11; Hebrews 11:10). At times, we may wobble as if our faith rests on shifting sand, but if we belong to Christ, our faith cannot ultimately fail because Christ, our Rock, can never fail. He's the wise architect, builder, and firm foundation of our faith. He designs our circumstances to build our faith, not tear it down. To make us strong in Him.

One day we'll stand together in His eternal kingdom in a city not built by human hands but by our Lord. In His kingdom, pain and sorrow cannot touch you. Until then, when your faith leans, lean into Christ (Romans 9:33).

When your faith is leaning, lean into Christ.

Consider the truths in today's reading and write a response to the following question.

> *If I truly believe and act on what God has revealed in this passage, how will the motivations and attitudes of my heart transform and my actions be different tomorrow?*

Pray and confess any areas of unbelief today's reading revealed. Ask God to open your eyes to understanding and believing His Word and for Him to empower you by His Spirit to obey and walk in the truth.

MEMORY VERSE

Recite this week's memory verse aloud five times:

Behold, his soul is puffed up; it is not upright within him, but the righteous shall live by his faith.

—HABAKKUK 2:4

TODAY'S READING

Habakkuk 2:2

INTENT

- The "vision" is God's prophecy concerning Judah's and Babylon's futures recorded in chapter 2 . . . and ultimately the future of all proud and righteous sinners.

TRUTH

Only twice in the Bible did God command someone to write on tablets. The first time was on Mount Sinai when God gave His law in fire and thunder. The next time was in today's reading.

Pray and study Habakkuk 2:2 in the chart. Note words or phrases that reveal the character, nature, and ways of God and that of anyone or anything else in the passage.

TRUTHS ABOUT GOD	VERSE	TRUTHS ABOUT OTHERS
	² And the LORD [Yahweh] answered me: "Write the vision; make it plain on tablets, so he may run who reads it."	

A Message to Endure Forever

Read Exodus 19:9–16. Consider the seriousness God placed on the moment He gave Israel His law on Mount Sinai. Notice His demands of holiness. What must happen to anyone who touched even the edge of the mountain?

In Habakkuk, God instructed His prophet to write a vision equal in importance to what He wrote with His finger on Mount Sinai.

"Write the vision; make it plain on tablets" (2:2).

Notice that the command isn't to write it onto scrolls but onto tablets. This message is to endure forever.

The essence of the vision is the gospel of Jesus Christ. (We'll see this in Habakkuk 2:4. Stay tuned.)

Jesus, the righteous Judge and Defender of His people, will come with judgment on proud sinners and with healing and salvation for those who will trust in Him.

The Gospel of Peace

This most important vision pointed Judah to the day when God's righteousness would meet His mercy and save them from Babylon. It spoke peace to all in Judah who would believe God and live by faith—whether in Jerusalem or Babylon.

Ultimately, the vision pointed to Jesus, when God's righteousness would meet His mercy on the cross. It speaks peace to every generation who will believe Christ's message of salvation by faith alone. This gospel message endures forever.

But there's another side to the vision (and gospel). Judgment comes to the proud sinner who refuses to believe. Their unbelief condemns them, whether in Jerusalem, Babylon, or in all the world.

"Whoever believes in him [Jesus] is not condemned, but whoever does not believe is condemned already, because he has not believed in the name of the only Son of God" (John 3:18).

God's perfect law written on the first tablets was never intended to save anyone because no one could ever perfectly keep the whole law. (Remember, we're not sinners because we sin. We sin because we're sinners.)

God intended the law to reveal our need for salvation and for Jesus, the only one who perfectly kept the whole law, that we may be saved from our unbelief and sin.

Read 1 Timothy 1:12–17.

Do you ache over lingering rebellion and unbelief in your own heart or in the heart of someone you love? (Yes, we Christians can still struggle with rebellion and unbelief.) Remember how the gospel transformed Paul—a man who once murderously opposed Christ, His Savior. Let his testimony infuse you with hope.

Stop and pray for the gospel of peace to break through even the darkest rebellion and unbelief in your heart and in those you love. Ask God to reveal any areas of ignorance and to replace them with belief. Remember as you pray that the power of the gospel is the power of God, not man (Romans 1:16). Do not fear. Believe.

Run

In the days of the ancient kings, messengers ran to proclaim the word of their sovereign. Prophets were sometimes pictured as running to proclaim the Word of the Lord (2 Kings 4:26; Zechariah 2:4).

What did God say was the purpose of Habakkuk's making the writing "plain"?

_____

Write out Ephesians 6:15.

_____

_____

The good news of the gospel gives us sure-footed peace even in times of trouble—peace with God and the peace of God. Even if our world topples like Judah when Babylon arrived, if we have peace with

God and the peace of God engraved in the tablets of our hearts, we can stand in the turmoil without despair.

God has made His vision—the gospel of peace—plain to us so that we will run to share this enduring message. May God give us more love so we'll strap on running shoes rather than bedroom slippers and run with the message that there is life, peace, and joy in Christ alone.

Read Isaiah 52:7.

Isaiah wrote of the day when God's messengers would run and declare peace in Jerusalem and freedom from Babylon. This glorious declaration pointed beyond their day to the cross of Christ when He would proclaim peace to all His children in every generation with three words: "It is finished" (John 19:30).

TRANSFORMATION

Jesus is our peace. "But now in Christ Jesus you who once were far off have been brought near by the blood of Christ. For he himself is our peace, who has made us both one and has broken down in his flesh the dividing wall of hostility by abolishing the law of commandments expressed in ordinances, that he might create in himself one new man in place of the two, so making peace" (Ephesians 2:13–15). The vision Habakkuk inscribed onto tablets brought hope to Judah and pointed to the day when Christ would do what the first tablets could never do—bring everlasting salvation and enduring peace.

The storms around us may disturb our peace, but they can never remove Christ's peace within us.

His peace is enduring, but we are forgetful.

His peace is unchanging, but we are prone to doubt.

Etch the truth of Christ's peace onto your heart so that no matter the storms that tempt you to panic, you'll live each day in His surpassing peace.

> And the peace of God, which surpasses all understanding, will guard your hearts and your minds in Christ Jesus.
>
> **PHILIPPIANS 4:7**

TRANSFORMATIONAL TRUTH

The storms around us can't remove Christ's peace within us.

Consider the truths in today's reading and write a response to the following question.

If I truly believe and act on what God has revealed in this passage, how will the motivations and attitudes of my heart transform and my actions be different tomorrow?

_____

_____

Pray and confess any areas of unbelief today's reading revealed. Ask God to open your eyes to understanding and believing His Word, and for Him to empower you by His Spirit to obey and walk in the truth.

MEMORY VERSE

Write out this week's memory verse: Habakkuk 2:4.

TODAY'S READING

Habakkuk 2:3

INTENT

- God is still speaking to Habakkuk about His prophecy recorded in Habakkuk 2.

TRUTH

Ever been packed and ready to head out for a much-anticipated dream vacation just to have it canceled hours before? Or made an offer on a house minutes after someone else put a contract on it? Or had the doctor say he needs "to see you right away" not long after your mom passed away from cancer? I've experienced all three.

God has appointed all things *in* their time, *for* their time, right *on* time. Blessed be the name of the Lord.

Pray and study Habakkuk 2:3 in the chart. Note words or phrases that reveal the character, nature, and ways of God and that of anyone or anything else in the passage.

TRUTHS ABOUT GOD	VERSE	TRUTHS ABOUT OTHERS
	³ For still the vision awaits its appointed time; it hastens to the end—it will not lie. If it seems slow, wait for it; it will surely come; it will not delay.	

God Never Scrambles

God's vision will not delay. It hastens to the end. It yearns for its fulfillment because God yearns for His kingdom to come. He yearned for Judah's salvation even more than Habakkuk did. Certainly, more than Judah did.

Judah wanted relief. God wanted their souls.

Only the Lord knows how long each trial must last to accomplish His eternal purposes. He will not fail or be delayed. He's not a tinkerer, trying out options and forming new ideas based on our actions and reactions. He has no planning committee tossing Him suggestions. He never bemoans, "I had such great plans, but you blew it. You've tied my hands. Now I'm powerless to help."

God never scrambles.

All Things *in* Their Time

"Rabbi, who sinned, this man or his parents, that he was born blind?" (John 9:2).

Jesus's disciples wrongly believed the same as most men of their time. People who prospered were righteous. Those who suffered were sinners.

Read John 9:1–7, 32.

What reason did Jesus give for why the man in this passage was born blind?

_____

Note the progression of spiritual sight this man received. Write down the words he used to refer to Jesus.

• Verse 11

_____

• Verse 17

_____

- Verse 38

God ordained for this man to be born blind in a world that shunned the blind and left them to beg. He ordained that he would live blind into adulthood before Christ would come and give him sight.

Does this seem cruel?

If we knew everything God knows, we'd do everything He does, exactly how He does it.

The man's blindness led to the opportunity for Christ to give him physical sight and—even better—spiritual sight. To testify to the truth of who Jesus is—the long-awaited Messiah and the blind man's Savior.

This man came to know Jesus in a way few have. He understood the power and majesty of Jesus in a way most of us can't until heaven. Never—before or since—has anyone given sight to a person born blind except Jesus.

The vision God gave Habakkuk had been appointed from eternity past to be given to Judah in this time of history. God didn't create this vision as a reaction to their sin. He wasn't scrambling. He was fulfilling His eternal plans in their time.

All Things *for* Their Time

Our suffering matters to God. He doesn't allow pain in our lives longer than is necessary to fulfill His good purposes for it. Will we be patient and wait for Him to work out His will in our life? Or will we put a deadline on Him to bless us? If we deem He failed to bless us as He should, will we then walk away or live like He's abandoned us?

Read Luke 8:41–56.

In Jesus's day, the woman who bled wasn't allowed to worship at the temple because she was considered unclean. No one could enter her home or touch her without becoming unclean themselves.

She lived as an outcast, broken and poor, because of something she couldn't control.

How old was Jairus's daughter (v. 42)?

_____

We don't know how long Jairus's daughter had been sick, but it probably wasn't long. How long had the woman been bleeding (v. 43)?

_____

What did Jesus call the woman (v. 48)?

_____

Twelve years earlier a daughter was born in Jairus's home to great joy. In another home, a woman became unclean to her deep despair. From eternity past, God ordained that on this glorious day, Jesus would come to His two beloved daughters as Father, Healer, Redeemer, Restorer, Giver of peace, and the Resurrection and the Life.

Does your trial feel too long—like the woman who bled?

_____

_____

Does your trial feel too severe—like the little girl who was dying?

_____

_____

What might God be doing in you and through your trial and its duration?

_____

_____

_____

_____

Habakkuk had cried out to God because Judah had been evil for too long. God was responding too slowly. Now it seemed He was responding too severely. But Habakkuk determined to trust God. Seeking His wisdom and correction enabled Habakkuk to rest in the length and severity of their captivity in Babylon.

All Things Right *on* Time

"Martha said to Jesus, 'Lord, if you had been here, my brother would not have died'" (John 11:21). To put it another way, "Jesus, you're too late."

Read John 11:5–6. What did Jesus do when He received the news about Lazarus?

_____

Read verses 7–15.

Jesus's disciples worried for Jesus's safety from the Jews. He answered their fears in idioms of their day. He talked of walking in the day and night (vv. 9–10). Like us, they had basically twelve hours of day and twelve hours of night. Jesus said as long as He was walking in the "day" portion of His appointed time on earth, no man could harm Him no matter how hard they tried. (The Jews failed more than once to kill Him before the cross.) But when the appointed time came for Him to walk in the "night," He'd "fall" into their evil hands and go to the cross . . . just as God planned.

Why was Jesus glad He didn't arrive before Lazarus died?

_____

I once read through the four Gospels in search of a time when someone remained dead in Jesus's presence. I couldn't find one. Not even on the cross. Jesus gave up His life before the men hanging next to Him died. Jesus is the resurrection and the life.

Read John 11:17–53.

How long had God appointed Lazarus to be in the grave (vv. 17, 39)?

_____

Who did God orchestrate to witness the miracle (vv. 19, 31)?

_____

Why did God choose these witnesses (vv. 41–42)?

_____

God had ordained that Jesus would be crucified during Passover as the final and perfect Passover Lamb. The Jews wanted to wait until after Passover for fear of the crowds. How did God move the timetable forward to coincide with Passover (vv. 45–53; Luke 22:1–5)?

_____

_____

God told Habakkuk His vision "hastens to the end" but not because it was late (Habakkuk 2:3). "Hastens" expresses God's longing for the redemption of His children and the knowledge of His glory to cover the earth. And it will, right on time.

Whatever you're facing today, remember, no trial is ever random. No sorrow creeps past God's watchful eyes. The cares of this world will only last for a short time. The day is coming when Christ will wipe every tear from our eyes (Revelation 21:4). It will not delay.

God has appointed all things *in* their time, *for* their time, right *on* time.

TRANSFORMATION

Jesus is the beginning and the end. "I am the Alpha and the Omega, the first and the last, the beginning and the end" (Revelation 22:13). From eternity to eternity, Jesus does all things in their time, for their time, and right on time. His vision of establishing righteousness in His coming kingdom hastens to the end. It will not delay.

TRANSFORMATIONAL TRUTH

God has appointed all things *in* their time, *for* their time, right *on* time.

Consider the truths in Habakkuk 2:3 and write a response to the following question.

If I truly believe and act on what God has revealed in this passage, how will the motivations and attitudes of my heart transform and my actions be different tomorrow?

Pray and confess any areas of unbelief today's reading revealed. Ask God to open your eyes to understanding and believing His Word, and for Him to empower you by His Spirit to obey and walk in the truth.

Write out this week's memory verse: Habakkuk 2:4.

TODAY'S READING

Habakkuk 2:4

INTENT

- *Behold* means "Listen up! This is important."

TRUTH

Martin Luther, a sixteenth-century monk, hated God. Does this surprise you?

Luther hated God because He punished sinners, and Luther couldn't escape his sin.

"I tortured myself with prayer, fasting, vigils and freezing; the frost alone might have killed me. . . . What else did I seek by doing this but God, who was supposed to note my strict observance of the monastic order and my austere life? I constantly walked in a dream and lived in real idolatry, for I did not believe in Christ: I regarded Him only as a severe and terrible Judge portrayed as seated on a rainbow."[12]

But then God led proud Luther to meditate on Romans 1:17:

For in the gospel the righteousness of God is revealed—a righteousness that is by faith from first to last, just as it is written: "The righteous will live by faith." (NIV)

Pray and study Habakkuk 2:4 in the chart. Note words or phrases that reveal the character, nature, and ways of God and that of anyone or anything else in the passage.

TRUTHS ABOUT GOD	VERSE	TRUTHS ABOUT OTHERS
	[4] Behold, his soul is puffed up; it is not upright within him, but the righteous shall live by his faith.	

Proud Sinners Exalt Themselves

Pride is a sin and the root of every other sin.

Which means, when we sin, we're guilty of at least two sins—the sin we committed and the sin of pride that led us to the sin we committed.

The sin of pride opposes God and His ways. It says, "My way, not God's way, is the best way." Sin's prideful nature permeates us from birth. We don't just act prideful. We are prideful. We're "puffed up" with pride. The original word for "puffed up" in today's verse is especially fitting because it also means "tumorous growth."[13]

Apart from Christ, we're hopeless. We can't improve ourselves any more than a tumor can improve itself. The proud remain prideful. Unless an outside force comes against the tumor, it remains a tumor. Some tumors grow and eventually destroy their host. All pride destroys.

The author of Hebrews made an important distinction when he said, "But my righteous one shall live by faith, and if he shrinks back, my soul has no pleasure in him" (10:38). Even if we attend church and teach Bible study, apart from Christ, our pride will exalt itself and shrink back from worshipping God.

Tumorous pride will never willingly let us humble ourselves before anyone or seek salvation outside of ourselves.

Write out James 4:6.

_____

_____

_____

Pray through Jeremiah 9:23–24.

Righteous Sinners Live by Faith

A "righteous sinner" sounds like an oxymoron, but this is the glorious promise of today's verse. As proud sinners, we were bloated in unrighteousness. But by God's merciful grace through faith in Christ, He removed our unrighteousness and credited us with Christ's righteousness. He permanently changed our legal status from "unrighteous" to "righteous."

We did nothing to earn this irrevocable pardon. We certainly didn't keep God's law. Our tumorous pride refuses to submit to God's commands. As Paul said, "Clearly no one who relies on the law is justified before God, because 'the righteous will live by faith'" (Galatians 3:11 NIV).

Christ did it all. He transformed us from "enemies" of God who fight against His will to "children of God" who seek to please Him (Romans 5:10; John 1:12).

So can we drop the "sinner" label now? Sadly, not yet.

At salvation Christ makes us into a new creation (Romans 11:29; 2 Corinthians 5:17), but He doesn't remove the sin that tempts us or our ability to sin. We still fall into old sinful habits and pride. But in Christ, we're "righteous sinners." (This is not to say our sin is righteous. Sin is never righteous.)

This wonderful truth brings us to the unique beauty of today's verse—its superabundant and glorious promise: The faith God gave to save us is the same faith by which we live. Our unfailing Christ still does it all.

Write out Romans 1:17.

_____

_____

_____

_____

Just as we couldn't save ourselves apart from Christ, we can't live a righteous life apart from Him. He must—and does—do it all.

Read Hebrews 13:20–21. According to this passage, who equips us to do God's will?

_____

How are we equipped?

_____

What are we equipped to do?

_____

Read Philippians 2:12–13. Write out verse 13.

_____

_____

Much of our frustration as Christians comes because we try to live the Christian life by our own efforts. When we read in Philippians 2:12 that we are to "work out [our] own salvation with fear and trembling," most of us double down and try harder.

But Paul's message isn't that we need more grit to be successful. Instead, Paul instructs us to live by the same kind of faith that saved us—Christ-did-it-all faith. We're to work out *through* our lives what Christ worked *into* us at salvation.

Christ works on our heart. We work on our feet. We walk in obedience to Christ and His Word.

As Good as Done

Habakkuk 2:4 is a truth and a promise.

Proud sinners *will* exalt themselves because it's pride's nature.

The righteous sinner *will* live by faith because Christ promised to do it all. It's His nature never to fail. What He promises is as good as done.

Read Joshua 5:13–15; 6:1–5. (Note: The commander of the Lord's army is a *Christophany*, an Old Testament appearance of Jesus.)

Circle the verb tense the Lord used in Joshua 6:2.

- Future—*I will give.*
- Present—*I am giving.*
- Past—*I have given.*

Why do you think He chose this particular verb tense?

_____

_____

When Joshua asked if the man was for or against Israel, Jesus simply said, "No." As I once heard someone say, Jesus didn't come to take sides. He came to take over. Or more accurately, to reveal that He already had.

God writes history in advance.

Jericho's king still sat on the throne, but God—our ultimate ruler—had already given Jericho to Israel. It was simply a matter of notifying Israel of their move-in date and method. God wasn't handing Israel the key to Jericho's front door. He was bringing Jericho's walls down.

Habakkuk knew this history. So when the Lord declared He'd given the nation of Judah to Babylon, Habakkuk could consider it done. And when God promised the righteous shall live by faith, Habakkuk could echo Christ on the cross, "It is finished."

Is there an old sinful habit you're stumbling over? Rather than believe the lie, "I'll never change," walk in the truth that Christ is your power to obey.

_____

_____

There's no situation we can face in which Jesus, the commander of the Lord's army, has not already gone before us. No circumstance which He does not already know its outcome and its ultimate good for us and His glory. Trust and obey.

TRANSFORMATION

Jesus is the commander of the Lord's army (Joshua 5:14). Christ has come and is coming again. He rules and leads His people in righteousness. Let us follow Him wherever He leads.

Instead of God being the harsh Judge he'd imagined, Martin Luther discovered God is the God of grace. And He's promised that the righteous will live by faith, and by faith in Christ, the righteous will truly live. He's the commander of the Lord's army. He will do it.

The righteous will live by faith, and by faith they'll truly live.

Consider the truths in Habakkuk 2:4 and write a response to the following question.

If I truly believe and act on what God has revealed in this passage, how will the motivations and attitudes of my heart transform and my actions be different tomorrow?

_____

_____

Pray and confess any areas of unbelief today's reading revealed. Ask God to open your eyes to understanding and believing His Word and for Him to empower you by His Spirit to obey and walk in the truth.

MEMORY VERSE

Write out this week's memory verse: Habakkuk 2:4.

TODAY'S READING

Habakkuk 2:5

INTENT

• "Moreover" points to the proud in the beginning of Habakkuk 2:4. The proud in this passage are specifically Babylon, who was drunk with the spoils they plundered and the power they possessed. The truths also apply to every proud person today.

• Habakkuk illustrates sin by personifying "wine," which fuels and betrays the proud and lures them to their death with its lies.

• "Sheol" in today's reading appears in some translations as "grave" or "hell." In other words, the realm of the dead.

TRUTH

Ever said something you instantly regretted? Or regretted later?

Ever betrayed a friend or a loved one?

I hate that I can say yes to both.

I also hate that I carry regrets I don't even know about because wine and something called "hunch punch" in my school days betrayed me. It promised fun but delivered deep misery and shame.

Why didn't I see the truth about the lies?

Pray and study Habakkuk 2:5 in the chart. Note words or phrases that reveal the character, nature, and ways of God and that of anyone or anything else in the passage.

TRUTHS ABOUT GOD	VERSE	TRUTHS ABOUT OTHERS
	[5] Moreover, wine is a traitor, an arrogant man who is never at rest. His greed is as wide as Sheol; like death he has never enough. He gathers for himself all nations and collects as his own all peoples.	

Sin Deludes

Like wine, sin corrupts our thinking. It deludes us into believing and embracing the most ridiculous—and even heinous—lies.

"What will you give me if I deliver him over to you?" (Matthew 26:15).

Sin's greatest delusion had begun . . . and it only cost the Pharisees thirty pieces of silver.

Judas believed that betraying Jesus would bring him more than Jesus offered. Judas wanted a different kind of Messiah. One who would exalt him to power.

Sin drives our pride and directs us to where it wants us to go—into every delusion and evil.

"It's just this one time."

"Everyone else is doing it."

"No one will get hurt."

Sin Is Never Satisfied

Like the drunk who never tells the bartender, "Thank you, but I've had enough," Babylon lusted after more. Their sin could never satisfy them because sin's appetite only enlarges. It must have more.

Babylon's insatiable and deluded appetite drove it to sink so low they committed unspeakable atrocities with delight. Sin and Satan have no limits to their depravity. The monstrous crimes of child molestation and human trafficking prove this.

Four Slippery Steps to Sin

Sin is evil beyond our imagination, and the slide into sin is often subtle.

Sin looks for weaknesses in our defenses. It will never give up until it's broken through—or until we soundly defeat it with truth.

We need to be wise to sin's tactics and never think we're above falling for its lies. If we think we're not susceptible, we're already deluded . . . at least a little.

James reveals how sin ensnares us in four slippery steps.

Read James 1:14–16.

Consider the four-step progression of sin we see in verses 14–15.

1. Our own evil desires entice us.
2. These sinful desires move us to conceive a plan of action.
3. Our actions give birth to sin.
4. Sin brings death.

Let's apply these four steps to Adam and Eve's slide into sin (Genesis 3:1–6).

1. Adam and Eve's evil desires enticed them.

Sin starts in the mind as a tempting thought when we're enticed by our own evil desires.

Adam and Eve saw the delicious-looking fruit and wanted it more than they wanted to please God. They may have imagined its taste would satisfy them more than God's goodness. They considered the serpent's words, "You will be like God." Their prideful desire to be equal with God hungered for the twisted version of truth (aka the lie) the serpent dangled before them.

2. Adam and Eve's evil desires moved them to conceive a plan of action.

Sin transforms our tempting thoughts into a specific plan of action.

Eve formed an instant plan to pluck the fruit off the tree and eat it. Adam chose not to intervene and stop Eve but rather to accept the fruit from her hand and eat it.

3. Adam and Eve's actions gave birth to sin.

Like Adam and Eve, our rebellious actions give birth to sin.

Adam and Eve rebelled against God, took the fruit, and ate what God had forbidden.

4. Sin killed them.

Sin, fully grown, brings death—but not always physical death. Sometimes it's the death of a relationship, reputation, or position. Most importantly, apart from salvation in Christ, sin brings eternal death.

When Adam and Eve sinned, they died spiritually. They died physically later. And their relationship with each other suffered. As did every relationship afterward.

Truth Breaks Sin's Grip

Sinful thoughts (aka lies) come from our inner desires as well as outside influences, like our culture. Truth breaks their grip no matter where they come from.

- **Sin's lie:** You deserve to be happy.
  Truth: We deserve hell, but in Christ we receive eternal life and abiding joy.
- **Sin's lie:** You can do whatever you want, and no one can judge you.
  Truth: Christ, the righteous Judge of all the earth, calls us to obey His commands. We'll all answer to Him on the Day of Judgment. None will escape.
- **Sin's lie:** You have to find your own truth.
  Truth: There's no truth but God's truth.

What other popular lies have you heard?

_____

_____

Which lies are you most susceptible to believing? What truths make the lies lose their grip?

_____

_____

Read 2 Corinthians 10:3–5. What does Paul tell us breaks sin's grip (v. 5)?

_____

When Babylon came, drunk with lust and power, they took God's people into captivity. God sent even His faithful servants into Babylon, but His truth protected their hearts and minds from sin's delusions and control. Men like Habakkuk, Daniel, Shadrach, Meshach, and Abednego took every thought captive and made it obey the truth. Even as God exalted them into the highest levels of government in Babylon, they held on to the truth. Those in Judah who believed the lies rejected God's Word, fell for sin's delusions, and suffered great loss under sin's control.

TRANSFORMATION

Jesus is the truth (John 14:6). Every thought, word, and deed that has ever been thought, uttered, or acted upon by Jesus is born out of and goes forth in truth. Likewise, every thought, word, and deed that's ever been thought, uttered, or acted upon that's true is born out of Christ.

We don't have to believe in Jesus to know and believe truth. Satan believes the truth that Christ is God. And he hates the truth. The forces of darkness seek to draw us away from the truth by making us drunk on their lies. They serve their lies up in the most attractive fashion. But when we hold on to Jesus, all their lies lose their magnetism and their grip.

TRANSFORMATIONAL TRUTH

Lies lose their grip when we hold on to truth.

Consider the truths in today's reading and write a response to the following question.

If I truly believe and act on what God has revealed in this passage, how will the motivations and attitudes of my heart transform and my actions be different tomorrow?

Pray and confess any areas of unbelief today's reading revealed. Ask God to open your eyes to understanding and believing His Word, and for Him to empower you by His Spirit to obey and walk in the truth.

MEMORY VERSE

Recite or write out each week's memory verse:
Habakkuk 2:14; 1:5; 1:12; 2:4.

Group Study Questions

LIVING BY FAITH: HABAKKUK 2:1-5

- What stood out most to you from this week's lessons? How did it impact you?

- Share a time this week you were able to ask yourself the two "Searching Questions." What did you learn from either question?

  Lord, what do I not know about you right now that I need to know?

  Lord, what do I not believe about you right now that I need to believe?

- The man Jesus healed in John 9 lived into adulthood as a blind man. Can you think of someone you know who's suffered publicly but been joyful in the Lord? Brainstorm truths they might know about God that have enabled them to trust Him in their suffering.

- Share a practical example of what it looks like for the righteous to live by Christ-did-it-all faith.

- On day 5 we looked at sin's four-step progression. Work through the progression displayed in another act of sin in the Bible such as David with Bathsheba (2 Samuel 11), Jacob tricking Isaac (Genesis 27), or the crucifixion of Christ (Mark 15).

- Which attribute of Christ most encouraged you this week?

BREAK UP INTO GROUPS OF TWO OR THREE.

Practice your memory verse with each other, share prayer requests, and pray for each other.

> Behold, his soul is puffed up; it is not upright within him,
> but the righteous shall live by his faith.
>
> **—HABAKKUK 2:4**

defeating

pride

HABAKKUK 2:6-20

TODAY'S READING

Habakkuk 2:6–8

INTENT

- **Taunt Song:** A taunt song is used as a public mocking (a taunting proverb) of impending doom to be remembered and sung by its audience. Some commentators see it as a lament. Others see it more like an ancient, "Take that!"

- **Woe:** In Hebrew, the word *woe* comes from a funeral lament and means "Ah!" or "Alas!" It's often used as a declaration of judgment. God proclaimed five woes in Habakkuk 2 against Babylon, every unrepentant sinner in every generation, and our fiercest enemy—Satan and his kingdom of darkness. We'll look at one woe each day this week.

- Habakkuk's audience would have understood these woes to be a prophecy of what they'd endure at the hands of Babylon as well as the judgment God promised would come upon Babylon at His appointed time. We have the benefit of reading both the prophecy of Judah's exile to Babylon in Habakkuk and the fulfillment of it in Daniel. The New Testament gives us a picture of the prophecy's even greater fulfillment in Christ.

- The first woe condemns Babylon's insatiable lust for power, heaping up wealth, success, and glory at others' expense.

- **Pledges:** Some translate the original word for *pledges* as heavy, "thick clay." Either way, the proud will sink before God under the weight of sin's debt.

- **Debtor:** The original word for *debtor* also means "bite," like the bite of a viper. How fitting.

- **Tremble:** The verb for *tremble* suggests a violent shaking, like a mafia shakedown when you didn't pay them your debt. You don't return from that.
- **Remnant:** Throughout the Bible, the remnant refers to those who continue to follow the Lord—the righteous.

TRUTH

More conquest. More wealth. More power. More. More. More.

Babylon's King Nebuchadnezzar built his glory and kingdom by violence and plunder. He heaped what wasn't his and amassed wealth by the blood of his enemies.

In arrogance, when he conquered Judah, he stole the gold and silver from God's temple and brought the sacred vessels into the house of his god. And he dragged Judah's finest back to Babylon—men like Daniel, Shadrach, Meshach, and Abednego.

Woe to the insatiable, who lust after power, position, and possessions. God will cause their evil to fall back on themselves.

Pray and study Habakkuk 2:6–8 in the chart. Note words or phrases that reveal the character, nature, and ways of God and that of anyone or anything else in the passage.

TRUTHS ABOUT GOD	VERSE	TRUTHS ABOUT OTHERS
	6 Shall not all these take up their taunt against him, with scoffing and riddles for him, and say, "Woe to him who heaps up what is not his own— for how long?— and loads himself with pledges!"	
	7 Will not your debtors suddenly arise, and those awake who will make you tremble? Then you will be spoil for them.	
	8 Because you have plundered many nations, all the remnant of the peoples shall plunder you, for the blood of man and violence to the earth, to cities and all who dwell in them.	

The Insatiable Heap but Can't Keep

Insatiable lust for power drove Nebuchadnezzar. It drives every proud sinner because sin is a vacuous hole. It can never be satisfied. The insatiable grab whatever they can from whoever can't stop them until they've met their match—or their end.

No matter what it looks like, the insatiable get away with nothing. Habakkuk warns they're like those who makes themselves rich by taking out loans. Eventually, they have to pay up with interest. God may allow plunderers to enjoy their spoils for a moment, but in the end, unrepentant sinners lose everything they've taken—and their souls.

Have you been "plundered"? What have you lost? Money? Health? Relationships? List anything that seems stolen from you.

_____

_____

_____

Which items on your list are a consequence of your own sin, pride, or unbelief? Confess and turn from your sin. God gives grace to the humble. Trust and believe.

_____

_____

Which items are a consequence of others' sins?

_____

_____

Pray for justice and trust God. Your suffering won't last a moment longer than He decrees is necessary (1 Thessalonians 4:1–8). God uses the suffering of the righteous to make us more like our radiant and merciful Lord and to bring us blessings in the end (Romans 8:28–29). It may not seem possible, but all things are possible with God.

Which items on your list are a result of living in a fallen world?

_____

_____

Pray for relief and strength to endure, and praise God where you are. He will not waste an ounce of your pain. Trust Him for heavenly treasures as He moves you toward His eternal kingdom where no one can plunder you again.

Which items on your list first passed through God's hands of love before they were allowed to touch you? And which ones must serve God's good purposes by His sovereign rule? (Hint: All of them.)

God Brings Down the Proud

Nebuchadnezzar impressed himself as he swept into Judah and conquered it with relative ease.

Read Daniel 1:1–4.

Who does this passage tell us is ultimately responsible for Nebuchadnezzar's success?

_____

There's nothing anyone has that they didn't receive from God (John 3:27). The Lord gives and takes away. Blessed be His name (Job 1:21).

Whenever God *gifts* the proud with success and possessions, we can be certain He's preparing to expose the worthlessness of their self-exalted glory and their idols. He's setting them up to bring them down to their knees in either repentance or judgment.

Whether we steal with our hands or in our hearts, if we build our success on the misery of others, the weight of our sin will crush us. If we repent, God will forgive us and lift us up (1 John 1:9).

God is pleased when we work to provide for our families and serve His kingdom. Plundering, on the other hand, is a problem. Let's wait on the unfailing kindness of the Lord. He sees our needs and cares.

Have you plundered instead of waiting for God to bless the work of your hands? Have you stolen from your employer whether in time or goods? Have you devoted worship to anyone or anything other than God? Where have you plundered?

_____

_____

_____

_____

Humble yourself and repent. Where possible, make amends. And trust God to deal with those who've plundered you. (When necessary, involve the judicial system. God established it to protect us.)

In Psalm 50:21, God promised that the wicked will be held accountable for all their actions. "These things you have done, and I have been silent; you thought that I was one like yourself. But now I rebuke you and lay the charge before you." Does this promise bring you comfort? If so, how?

_____

_____

Does your answer change when you consider God will hold them accountable in His timing, not ours?

_____

_____

Treasures Forever

Even the most faithful suffer lack—sometimes severe lack.

God has graciously given us a vivid reminder through the Israelites' forty years in the wilderness that we can trust Him with all our needs. He fed them bread from heaven, water from a rock, and their shoes and clothes never wore out. And yet they grumbled.

Whenever we complain about areas of lack in our life, we're like the Israelites. We're guilty of suggesting God isn't caring for us as He should. Of questioning His love and power. He controls everything and faithfully causes blessings and curses to work on His behalf to serve our ultimate good and His glory—even the insatiable's plundering.

Daniel, Shadrach, Meshach, and Abednego refused the king's food and wine. They hungered for the righteousness of God, not the treasures of Babylon. God gave them both.

Nebuchadnezzar exalted the men to the highest positions of power in his government because he "found them ten times better than all the magicians and enchanters that were in all his kingdom" (Daniel 1:20).

When we suffer like Daniel and his friends through no fault of our own, and we glorify God through it, we store up eternal rewards. Heavenly treasures shine brighter than any on earth—and no one can steal them.

Write out Matthew 6:19–21.

_____

_____

_____

_____

TRANSFORMATION

Jesus is our portion. "'The LORD is my portion,' says my soul, 'therefore I will hope in him'" (Lamentations 3:24). Jesus outshines every earthly treasure. Even if everything in this world is taken from us, Jesus is ours forever (Psalm 73:26).

The proud heap but can't keep. The righteous enjoy treasures forever.

The proud heap but can't keep. The righteous enjoy treasures forever.

Consider the truths in today's reading and write a response to the following question.

If I truly believe and act on what God has revealed in this passage, how will the motivations and attitudes of my heart transform and my actions be different tomorrow?

_____

_____

Pray and confess any areas of unbelief today's reading revealed. Ask God to open your eyes to understanding and believing His Word, and for Him to empower you by His Spirit to obey and walk in the truth.

MEMORY VERSE

Recite this week's memory verse aloud five times.

> What profit is an idol
>   when its maker has shaped it,
>   a metal image, a teacher of lies?
> For its maker trusts in his own creation
>   when he makes speechless idols!

—HABAKKUK 2:18

WEEK FIVE — *day two*

TODAY'S READING

Habakkuk 2:9–11

INTENT

- **The second woe** condemns Babylon's cruel method of rule designed to insulate themselves from any challenge to their power, wealth, and control.
- **Irony:** Habakkuk used irony throughout the five woes. In today's reading, Babylon devised plans to increase their wealth and glory. Ironically, God used these same plans to devise their ruin and shame. This applies to the proud of every generation.
- **Nests:** Ancient civilizations often built cities high on mountains and cliffs to protect themselves from invaders.
- **Cutting off:** Ancient rulers often killed ("cut off") the conquered kings and their family to protect themselves from the king's descendants avenging their death or claiming the throne.
- Isaiah shared the same message to the northern kingdom of Israel in Isaiah 10.

TRUTH

Daniel, God's faithful servant whether in Jerusalem or Babylon, slept better than his captor, Nebuchadnezzar. A nightmare jerked the king out of his sleep.

A statue of gold, silver, bronze, iron, and clay stood tall in Nebuchadnezzar's dream until a boulder hurtled down from heaven and obliterated the statue. The crushing stone transformed into a towering mountain and filled the earth (Daniel 2). Nebuchadnezzar trembled on his bed.

Woe to the insulated, who gather power, position, and possessions thinking they can shield themselves from threats to their comfort or their right to rule others or themselves.

Woe to the arrogant, who cut off those who would question or challenge their decisions and seek to make themselves untouchable—even from God.

Woe to them, for their evil will fall back on themselves.

Pray and study Habakkuk 2:9–11 in the chart. Note words or phrases that reveal the character, nature, and ways of God and that of anyone or anything else in the passage.

TRUTHS ABOUT GOD	VERSE	TRUTHS ABOUT OTHERS
	9 Woe to him who gets evil gain for his house, to set his nest on high, to be safe from the reach of harm!	
	10 You have devised shame for your house by cutting off many peoples; you have forfeited your life.	
	11 For the stone will cry out from the wall, and the beam from the woodwork respond.	

The Insulated Protect Themselves at Any Cost

The statue in Nebuchadnezzar's dream represented earthly kingdoms. The gold depicted the glorious—but eventually obliterated—kingdom of Babylon. The crushing stone was Christ the Lord.

Jesus will destroy every earthly kingdom represented by the statue. He's the mountain that will fill the earth when the kingdom of our Lord and Christ comes. And He shall reign forever and ever (Revelation 11:15).

But Nebuchadnezzar wanted *his* rule to reign forever.

At any cost.

Normally this would include killing the former king and his whole family. But Nebuchadnezzar didn't kill Judah's king, Zedekiah. Execution would have been too merciful. Instead, he forced Zedekiah to watch henchmen slaughter his sons. Then Nebuchadnezzar ordered the henchmen to gouge out Zedekiah's eyes so he would live the remainder of his life haunted by this last torturous sight.

It seems impossible that sin and pride could take anyone so far into the depths of cruelty, but this is the way of the insulated. They're not concerned with what's cruel, but with what's effective. They must keep their "dynasty" at any cost.

The insulated do unto others before others can do unto them.

The insulated today build fortresses in their "kingdoms" and minds, determined to secure unassailable sovereignty at any cost—which they never expect to pay. They expect everyone else to pay.

But one day God will bring down every fortress set against Him, and great will be their fall. At the same time, He'll lift up His downtrodden children and grant them eternal rest and delight.

Read Obadiah 3–4 and write out verse 4.

The Insulated Will Be Exposed

"What?" the insulated say to God. "I didn't do anything wrong."

If the fortresses of the insulated could talk, the stones from their walls would witness against them. The beams from their woodwork would speak out and broadcast their shame (see Habakkuk 2:11).

But stones and beams can't speak, so God exposes their sins and their hearts.

What about us? Are we determined to rule our personal kingdom and hold on to whatever power, position, or possessions we can? Are we tucking away our sins in hopes no one exposes them?

"Be sure your sin will find you out" (Numbers 32:23).

It will destroy us and those we love.

Let's examine our hearts and ask God to reveal if we display any harmful tendencies of the insulated. Here are a few:

- The insulated seek admiration and approval from others to build their fortress of self-worth. When they don't get it, they become angry, depressed, or withdrawn.
- They view even sincere questions as challenges to their intelligence or authority and a sign of disrespect.
- They make excuses for their harsh behavior, believing they would never have *had* to act or speak the way they did if the other person had respected them.

If we think pride isn't one of our main challenges, we're walking in darkness. But Christ's light pierces the darkness and brings revival. Every insulating tendency we develop to protect ourselves—to protect our pride—will ultimately betray us. When God calls us to account, He'll bring the truth to light.

The Insulated Run into Darkness

Before Babylon arrived in Jerusalem, God gave the nation of Judah a seemingly obvious choice.

Read Jeremiah 21:1–10.

God's people could believe His promise through Jeremiah, surrender to Babylon, and enjoy life. Or they could ignore His promise, stay in Jerusalem to fight, and die from war, famine, and disease.

Pride leads us into such delusion we'll actually run from truth and God's unfailing promises and into darkness and death. Woe to the proud (like Zedekiah and other Jews) who chose the curses and death.

Read Jeremiah 38:14–39:10. Zedekiah could have avoided his suffering if he'd surrendered. (See 38:17–23.) What do you think influenced Zedekiah's decision not to surrender?

The Righteous Dwell in Light

When I played hide-and-seek with friends, I loved it when their dog sniffed them out and gave away their best hiding spots. Pride may love the darkness, but Christ's Light is better than a hound dog.

This is the beauty of the sinner's new nature in Christ—it loves the Light.

Pride tries to convince us we prefer the darkness, but if we'll ignore our lying pride and walk in the Light, we'll discover we love the Holy Spirit shining into the corners of our heart. We'll delight when God orchestrates events to expose and clean out pride's best hiding spots. He humbles us because He wants to refine our hearts and revive us.

The Light of truth shines the grace of Christ into our hearts and restores us into His warm fellowship.

Pray through Isaiah 57:15.

For thus says the One who is high and lifted up,
　　who inhabits eternity, whose name is Holy:
"I dwell in the high and holy place,
　　and also with him who is of a contrite and lowly spirit,
to revive the spirit of the lowly,
　　and to revive the heart of the contrite."

Dear Christian, settle it forever in your heart that in your new nature in Christ, you love the Light. You do. Don't fall for pride's deceit.

Embrace your new nature, flee sin, and run to the Light where shame can't touch you and grace and mercy will always find you. Let God revive you and guard you—or set you free—from the hoarding tendencies of the insulated. Let's be more like Habakkuk—cling to God and hold all else lightly. It leads to rejoicing.

TRANSFORMATION

Jesus is the Light. "In him was life, and the life was the light of men. The light shines in the darkness, and the darkness has not overcome it" (John 1:4–5).

No darkness can hide from Christ or consume Him or His piercing Light. If you're in Christ, stand in the warmth of His Light and rejoice. You're safe in Him regardless of what's happening around you in the darkness. If you're far from Christ, turn from the darkness of sin today and believe in Him. Come to the Light and find life, eternal joy, and rest for your soul (Matthew 11:28–30).

TRANSFORMATIONAL TRUTH

Cling to God and hold all else lightly.

Consider the truths in today's reading and write a response to the following question.

If I truly believe and act on what God has revealed in this passage, how will the motivations and attitudes of my heart transform and my actions be different tomorrow?

Pray and confess any areas of unbelief today's reading revealed. Ask God to open your eyes to understanding and believing His Word, and for Him to empower you by His Spirit to obey and walk in the truth.

MEMORY VERSE

Write out this week's memory verse: Habakkuk 2:18.

TODAY'S READING

Habakkuk 2:12–14

INTENT

• **The third woe** condemns Babylon's tyranny—destroying others to gain for themselves. This prophecy exposed Babylon's lust for glory. Daniel recorded the inglorious events to King Nebuchadnezzar's lasting shame.

• When Habakkuk refers to "the glory of the Lord" (v. 14), his audience would have understood *glory* as the radiant sum of all His attributes—His holiness, love, goodness, mercy, wrath, grace, and every other of His resplendent characteristics.

TRUTH

Nebuchadnezzar's statue nightmare had both haunted and inspired him, or so it seems. Sometime after his dream, he ordered a towering statue of his own, but without the lesser materials of silver, bronze, iron, or clay. He covered his statue from head to toe in gold and set it up in Babylon for all to see and worship.

Just as Habakkuk had prophesied, Nebuchadnezzar founded his empire—his inglorious majesty—on blood and violence. But God would soon expose the truth about Nebuchadnezzar. The radiance of his glory couldn't fill a closet with light, much less the earth.

Pray and study Habakkuk 2:12–14 in the chart. Note words or phrases that reveal the character, nature, and ways of God and that of anyone or anything else in the passage.

TRUTHS ABOUT GOD	VERSE	TRUTHS ABOUT OTHERS
	^{12} Woe to him who builds a town with blood and founds a city on iniquity!	
	^{13} Behold, is it not from the Lord of hosts that peoples labor merely for fire, and nations weary themselves for nothing?	
	^{14} For the earth will be filled with the knowledge of the glory of the Lord as the waters cover the sea.	

The Inglorious Revel in Their Own Glory

The night of Nebuchadnezzar's dream, God's prophet Daniel revealed the meaning of the statue's materials. The gold represented his reign. The other materials represented the succeeding empires.

God had declared through Habakkuk that Babylon would conquer Judah. Through Daniel, He declared Babylon's golden rule would fall to a lesser kingdom—a kingdom more of the quality of silver, not gold.

Perhaps this is why Nebuchadnezzar covered his entire statue in gold. To proclaim his kingdom would never fall to anyone. We don't know.

We also don't know what the statue looked like. Did it resemble him? Or one of his gods? We do know, however, that he set it up to proclaim his majesty. At almost one hundred feet tall and eleven feet wide, it rivaled the height of his pride (Daniel 3:1).

Whenever the music played, if anyone in the city failed to fall down and worship his statue, he commanded they "immediately be cast into a burning fiery furnace" (v. 6).

Submit or scorch.

Are there areas in your life where you've set up a "statue" to your majesty? We can use just about anything to build a monument to our pride, from having the best garden to being the brightest in our field. In what areas of your life do you find yourself tempted to seek admiration from others?

_____

_____

_____

_____

The Inglorious Toil for Ashes

When the music played in Babylon, the people fell down and worshipped Nebuchadnezzar's statue—but not Shadrach, Meshach, and Abednego. The three Hebrew men stood tall.

The report of their defiance quickly reached Nebuchadnezzar and enflamed his already engorged pride. He demanded Shadrach, Meshach, and Abednego be brought before him.

He said, "If you do not worship, you shall immediately be cast into a burning fiery furnace. And who is the god who will deliver you out of my hands?" (v. 15).

The Hebrew men's response is one of my favorite passages. I long to display such unflinching faith.

O Nebuchadnezzar, we have no need to answer you in this matter. If this be so, our God whom we serve is able to deliver us from the burning fiery furnace, and he will deliver us out of your hand, O king. But if not, be it known to you, O king, that we will not serve your gods or worship the golden image that you have set up. (vv. 16–18)

Nebuchadnezzar responded by heating the furnace seven times hotter and ordering the soldiers to bind the men in ropes and toss them into the fire.

Nebuchadnezzar jumped up. "Did we not cast three men bound into the fire?"

"True, O king."

"But I see four men unbound, walking in the midst of the fire, and they are not hurt; and the appearance of the fourth is like a son of the gods" (vv. 24–25).

Many Bible scholars agree that the fourth was Jesus, the Son of Man and Son of the one true God.

Nebuchadnezzar approached the furnace and shouted, "Shadrach, Meshach, and Abednego, servants of the Most High God, come out, and come here!" (v. 26).

The three men stepped from the flames without even a hair on their head singed or their cloaks scorched. Not even the smell of smoke rested on them.

Only one thing burned in the fire. Did you notice it?
Nebuchadnezzar noticed. (See verses 20–21, 24–25.)

Only God can cause the things that bind us to burn away while leaving us untouched by the flames. We labor to build cities, towns, and monuments to our majesty, but even our best efforts are worthless. No better than kindling for a furnace.

But when we follow the Lord's leading and labor for His glory, we walk in His presence, unbound by inglorious pride. And our work will be revealed as gold, which survives a fire—like Shadrach, Meshach, and Abednego (1 Corinthians 3:10–15).

God's three faithful servants didn't seek their own glory in their bold stance. They didn't beat their chests and cry, "Look at us! We aren't afraid to defy authority." They simply refused to worship any other god but the one true God . . . no matter the cost.

God will not give His glory to another nor His praise to idols (Isaiah 42:8). In all our endeavors, we labor and tire ourselves for nothing if God's glory isn't our highest goal and greatest desire. Those who seek His glory above all will find that the things of this world that once held them in bondage turn to ash and fall away.

God Exposes the Inglorious

When Jesus prayed in the garden of Gethsemane, a report of His whereabouts reached the Jewish leaders. They sent Judas with a mob of soldiers to bind and arrest Jesus. The rope was unnecessary. Jesus had every intention of going with them quietly. Besides, no rope in heaven or earth can hold the Son of God without His permission.

Do you fret about your country's present condition? Or the governments or ruthless dictators in other countries? What does our fearful fretting reflect regarding our beliefs about God?

_____

_____

Consider your answer above and read Daniel 2:20–21. How does this impact your previous answer?

_____

_____

All who rule either seek to honor God, or they toil for nothing. At the right time, God will move. He will fulfill all His purposes for the time allowed for them to wield power. They will answer for their crimes. And by the providence and power of God, their majesty will only bring them shame . . . and bring glory to God.

Nebuchadnezzar intended his image of gold to display his glory. Instead, it exposed his ingloriousness and revealed God's power. In the end, Nebuchadnezzar conceded defeat and exalted the name of the Lord. Sadly, it's doubtful he gave up his other gods—his worthless idols—or repented of his pride for long.

The Righteous Display God's Glory

By God's decree, kingdoms rise and fall.

Babylon.

The Medes and the Persians.

Greece.

The iron rule of Rome.

Leaders toil and weary themselves to build a lasting dynasty, whether in government, business, or their own minds. But in the end only one kingdom and King will remain—the kingdom of God and Christ, our King.

Don't despair the days of the inglorious. The Glorious is coming.

Read about the doom of Babylon in Revelation 18:7–9. (Scholars debate exactly who this Babylon is in Revelation, but they agree "she" is obsessed with her own glory and a fierce enemy of God and His glory to her eternal destruction.)

TRANSFORMATION

Jesus is the glory of the Lord. "For the earth will be filled with the knowledge of the glory of the Lord as the waters cover the sea" (Habakkuk 2:14). Think about the fullness of this image.

When Christ returns, the entire earth will know and see the glory of the Lord. His glory will flood the earth and fill every crevice of doubt or denial.

All skepticism will end.

Every tongue will confess—either willingly or unwillingly—that Jesus Christ is Lord.

His authority and power will stand unquestioned.

Christ's glory will reign. Indestructible and indescribable.

"And the glory of the LORD shall be revealed, and all flesh shall see it together, for the mouth of the LORD has spoken" (Isaiah 40:5).

Don't despair the days of the inglorious.
The Glorious is coming.

Consider the truths in today's reading and write a response to the following question.

> *If I truly believe and act on what God has revealed in this passage, how will the motivations and attitudes of my heart transform and my actions be different tomorrow?*

_____

_____

Pray and confess any areas of unbelief today's reading revealed. Ask God to open your eyes to understanding and believing His Word, and for Him to empower you by His Spirit to obey and walk in the truth.

MEMORY VERSE

Write out this week's memory verse: Habakkuk 2:18.

TODAY'S READING

Habakkuk 2:15–17

INTENT

• **The fourth woe** condemns Babylon's cruel treatment of their captives as one who intentionally gets their neighbor drunk to delight in their shame.

• **To show themselves uncircumcised** was most shameful because it identified them as being separated from God.[14]

• **Lebanon** supplied wood for buildings and temples. Some commentators believe this verse declares a woe against Babylon's desecration of the earth in their razing of Lebanon's trees. Others believe it may refer to Babylon's razing of the temple in Jerusalem, which was built with Lebanon wood.

TRUTH

Nebuchadnezzar walked on the roof of his palace and gazed at his city. "Is not this great Babylon, which I have built by my mighty power as a royal residence and for the glory of my majesty?" (Daniel 4:30).

Woe to the intoxicated, drunk on their own glory and lusts. God will cause their evil to fall back on themselves.

Pray and study Habakkuk 2:15–17 in the chart. Note words or phrases that reveal the character, nature, and ways of God and that of anyone or anything else in the passage.

TRUTHS ABOUT GOD	VERSE	TRUTHS ABOUT OTHERS
	[15] Woe to him who makes his neighbors drink— you pour out your wrath and make them drunk, in order to gaze at their nakedness!	
	[16] You will have your fill of shame instead of glory. Drink, yourself, and show your uncircumcision! The cup in the Lord's right hand will come around to you, and utter shame will come upon your glory!	
	[17] The violence done to Lebanon will overwhelm you, as will the destruction of the beasts that terrified them, for the blood of man and violence to the earth, to cities and all who dwell in them.	

The Intoxicated See What They Want

Nebuchadnezzar saw what his prideful heart wanted him to see. Intoxicated by his own glory and lust for power, position, and possessions, he delighted in the violence he did to the earth, the cities, and all who dwelled in them.

He laughed at his enemies' humiliation as he dragged prisoners with hooks and plundered their belongings. He smirked as he defended his honor by tossing even his finest subjects into a raging fire like worthless trash.

He imagined glory crowned him, not shame.

But God knew how to sober him out of his drunken stupor.

Read Daniel 4:4–27.

One year before Nebuchadnezzar's narcissistic praise-fest on his rooftop, another nightmare had jolted him.

When Daniel interpreted the dream and Nebuchadnezzar's doom, he urged the king to turn from his sins and practice righteousness by showing mercy to those he'd oppressed. Perhaps God would relent and allow Nebuchadnezzar's prosperity to continue.

Perhaps.

We'll never know because Nebuchadnezzar ignored Daniel's urging. He was too intoxicated with pride. Like the religious rulers in Jesus's day.

For three years Jesus walked among His chosen nation Israel and revealed the truth of His divine majesty by His words and His works. But they hated Him. They crowned their Messiah and King with thorns and nailed Him to a cross—a vivid display of the violence of sin and pride.

God Sobers the Intoxicated

God had given Nebuchadnezzar a full year to repent and turn from his evil. He declined the offer to avoid humiliation. Instead, he lifted his praise to himself, not God.

"While the words were still in the king's mouth, there fell a voice from heaven" (Daniel 4:31).

Read Daniel 4:30–33. Sum up what the voice from heaven declared.

_____

_____

Nebuchadnezzar's appearance finally matched his true majesty. God transformed him into a mindless grass-eating, stringy-haired "animal" with claws for fingers.

Nebuchadnezzar thought no one ruled him. That he could force anyone to do whatever he wanted, laugh at their shame, and continue forever. But the cup in God's right hand—His cup of holy wrath—turned around toward Nebuchadnezzar's mouth.

The king's narcissistic pride had dragged him in his intoxicated stupor wherever it wanted him to go. At the appointed time, God dragged him into a field where he ate grass like an ox for seven years.

Those who are intoxicated by their own glory wind up groveling in their shame.

What did God say would cause Nebuchadnezzar's sanity to return to him? (Daniel 4:32)

_____

_____

What area in your life is the hardest to surrender to God's rule? How you spend your time? Your most important relationships? Why do you think this is?

_____

_____

God's Grace Removes Our Shame

Apart from Christ, our shame would remain forever. But in Him, His grace and mercy wash our guilt and shame away. In their place God fills us with abiding joy and hearts of gratitude because of what He's done for us—the righteous for the unrighteous (1 Peter 3:18).

Read Daniel 4:34–37.

Did the beginning of verse 34 catch your attention? "At the end of the days I, Nebuchadnezzar, lifted my eyes to heaven." Where had his gaze been before?

_____

Where is your gaze most often? (Hint: Where we spend the most time and money reveals the focus of our gaze.)

_____

_____

Write out Daniel 4:35.

_____

_____

_____

_____

_____

In God's extravagant grace and mercy, He restored more than Nebuchadnezzar's reason to him. He also restored his kingdom and made it even greater. Consider how remarkable this is. Without God's restraining hand, greedy men would've stumbled over each other to do away with the crazy king and claim his throne. But God didn't allow it.

No matter what we've endured—and some have endured horrors—it could still be worse because sin and Satan have zero mercy. Unspeakable evil is their delight. But God abounds in grace and mercy, and He is in control.

TRANSFORMATION

Jesus is the wellspring of life. He satisfies the deepest needs and longings of our souls now and forever. He offers living water that wells up in our souls like an ever-flowing spring of life and joy (John 4:14). Why do we seek our own glory when Christ's glory is in us wherever we go?

TRANSFORMATIONAL TRUTH

Those intoxicated by their own glory wind up sobered by their shame.

Consider the truths in today's reading and write a response to the following question.

> *If I truly believe and act on what God has revealed in this passage, how will the motivations and attitudes of my heart transform and my actions be different tomorrow?*

Pray and confess any areas of unbelief today's reading revealed. Ask God to open your eyes to understanding and believing His Word, and for Him to empower you by His Spirit to obey and walk in the truth.

MEMORY VERSE

Write out this week's memory verse: Habakkuk 2:18.

TODAY'S READING

Habakkuk 2:18–20

INTENT

• **The fifth woe** condemns Babylon's idolatry—the senseless and self-destructive worship of anyone or anything other than the one true God.

• This woe is mentioned in the middle of the decree, not the beginning like the others. God set it apart. If we pay attention to it—and obey it—we won't suffer the other woes.

• Habakkuk's audience understood that God's throne is in heaven, but He'd chosen to dwell among His people in His temple in Jerusalem (v. 20). Unfortunately, like Babylon, Judah foolishly bowed before lifeless idols they'd made with their own hands (vv. 18–19).

• Habakkuk prophesied that Judah would be exiled in idolatrous Babylon. During Judah's exile, Babylon committed the acts this passage warned against and sealed their own ruin.

• God intended Habakkuk's words to speak to all generations who worship anyone or anything other than Him.

TRUTH

Babylon's final king, Belshazzar, hosted an elaborate feast for a thousand lords. He was too busy attending to his guests and his drinking to notice the events transpiring outside his city walls (Daniel 5:1).

Habakkuk prophesied Babylon's judgment. The time had come. And so had the Medes and the Persians. Judah's seventy-year exile was coming to an end.

Oblivious of his impending doom, Belshazzar called for the gold and silver cups that Nebuchadnezzar had taken from the temple of God. He and his drunken guests filled God's sacred cups with wine and toasted to their "gods of silver and gold, of bronze, iron, wood, and stone, which do not see or hear or know" (v. 23).

They mocked the one true God who sees, hears, and knows all things—and who held their lives in His hands.

Woe to the idolater; they revere worthless affections to their demise. God will cause their evil to fall back on themselves.

Pray and study Habakkuk 2:18–20 in the chart. Note words or phrases that reveal the character, nature, and ways of God and that of anyone or anything else in the passage.

TRUTHS ABOUT GOD	VERSE	TRUTHS ABOUT OTHERS
	18 What profit is an idol when its maker has shaped it, a metal image, a teacher of lies? For its maker trusts in his own creation when he makes speechless idols!	
	19 Woe to him who says to a wooden thing, Awake; to a silent stone, Arise! Can this teach? Behold, it is overlaid with gold and silver, and there is no breath at all in it.	
	20 But the Lord is in his holy temple; let all the earth keep silence before him.	

Idolaters Reflect What They Revere

Seventy years before Belshazzar's feast (in the days of Habakkuk), the nation of Judah fell under God's judgment because they'd revered worthless idols—which led to other sins. At the appointed time, God silenced Judah's boasting by sending them to Babylon.

But worse than Judah, Babylon worshipped ruthless gods of their own making and reflected them in violence beyond compare.

God would now silence Babylon.

After Belshazzar and his guests toasted their gods, the finger of a human hand appeared and wrote on the wall of the king's palace (Daniel 5:5).

Panic seized Belshazzar.

The guests stared dumbfounded. (Much like their dumb gods—unable to speak or think.)

Belshazzar called for his enchanters, magicians, and astrologers. He promised royal clothing, gold chains, and power if they could interpret the writing.

They couldn't read it, much less interpret it. Their wisdom matched their gods'.

But Daniel could.

Daniel read the writing on the wall. "Mene, Mene, Tekel, and Parsin" (v. 25).

And he interpreted its meaning.

"Mene, God has numbered the days of your kingdom and brought it to an end; Tekel, you have been weighed in the balances and found wanting; Peres, your kingdom is divided and given to the Medes and Persians" (vv. 26–28).

The idols Babylon worshipped couldn't stop God's hand. The Lord had already positioned Babylon's downfall outside their gates, blocking the river that ran under their impregnable walls and into their cherished city.

In what ways did Belshazzar and Daniel reflect what they revered?

_____

_____

_____

Read Psalm 115:1–8. Write out verse 8.

_____

_____

Idols Are Lifeless . . . and Deadly

Idols are lifeless entities and not true gods. Some may be physical like money, others as obsessions in our minds like fame. Neither have breath or actual power. They're deaf and dumb, but not harmless.

Biblical scholar G. K. Beale said, "Behind the idols, it's not just nothing, it's spiritual death and demons!"[15]

Habakkuk called the man-made image that the proud shaped, "a teacher of lies" (Habakkuk 2:18). Jesus called Satan a "liar" and the "father of lies." He said there's "no truth in him" (John 8:44). This explains why idol makers trust in their own creations—such faith is insanity from Satan.

John Calvin called our minds "a perpetual forge of idols."[16] In other words, our minds are idol-making factories. The prophet Jeremiah said, "The heart is deceitful above all things, and desperately sick; who can understand it?" (Jeremiah 17:9).

Exactly.

One indicator we may be worshipping an idol is when our behavior contradicts Scripture.

If we panic when we make a mistake, we may be worshipping the idol of perfectionism rather than the God of all peace.

If we grow anxious when our bills come due, we may be worshipping the idol of security rather than the God who cares for His children.

What idols tempt you? Admiration? A hefty bank account? A perfect marriage?

_____

_____

What lies do your idols tell? Write some down—and then scratch them out and replace them with truth.

_____

_____

_____

_____

_____

We can't forsake idols we don't realize we've created or reject lies we don't realize we believe. Christ and His Word are the cure. His Light forces the lies into the open.

Know the Word. The whole Word.

And pray.

God's Spirit is our teacher. He will lead us into all truth through His Word.

The Earth Will Be Silent before God

Belshazzar revered his idols. When Daniel spoke the word of the Lord to him, he became as deaf and speechless as his gods. Rather than humble his heart, Belshazzar hardened it. He refused to listen to the Lord—and was silenced in the end.

"That very night Belshazzar the Chaldean king was killed. And Darius the Mede received the kingdom" (Daniel 5:30–31).

If the whole world refused to worship God, He'd still reign and rule in His holy temple, Lord over all. He doesn't need us or our praise. We need Him. Our souls need to worship Him, and Him alone.

Fortunately, the whole world will not all turn away from worshipping God because Christ preserves His church. He holds us secure and is purifying us and our worship.

The day is coming when the earth will keep silent before God when Christ returns. All boasting will end and the Truth will stand before the earth unchallenged.

Why will you keep silent when Christ returns? From anguish because you rejected Christ and His salvation? Or from awe of the grace that saved you? We must all answer this question one day. Journal your thoughts.

_____

_____

_____

_____

_____

_____

_____

The Righteous Revere—and Reflect—the Lord

When we left Daniel, Belshazzar had dressed him in a robe worthy of a king as a reward for interpreting the writing on the wall, ironically for prophesying his demise. That very night the Medes and Persians waltzed up the dry riverbed, conquered Babylon, and killed Belshazzar.

Read Daniel 6:1–2. What happened to Daniel next?

_____

Daniel faithfully served whoever God called him to serve—even Babylon's godless rulers. Idolatry surrounded him, but he never succumbed to it. He revered the Lord alone as God and his supreme authority. By God's grace, Daniel received honor from the godless kings he served and eternal treasures in heaven.

If you're not where you want to be in your walk with Christ, never accept the lie that you can't change. The presence of God's Spirit and His Word in Christians makes our hearts softer, more moldable, and more compliant to His will—able to trust God like Daniel and Habakkuk. Soak in His Word. Study it. Memorize it. Live it.

As we regard the Lord in His Word and revere Him in our worship, we'll reflect Him in our lives.

Read 2 Corinthians 3:16–18.

TRANSFORMATION

Jesus is God, the Great I am. "Truly, truly, I say to you, before Abraham was, I am" (John 8:58). Jesus is the one true God and everything we'll ever need for every moment—the Great I am. Idols are the Great I Am Not. They are not God. They are not the way, the truth, or the life. They are nothing they promise to be. But Jesus is. He's more than our minds could ever imagine.

We reflect what we revere.

Consider the truths in today's reading and write a response to the following question.

> *If I truly believe and act on what God has revealed in this passage, how will the motivations and attitudes of my heart transform and my actions be different tomorrow?*

_____

_____

Pray and confess any areas of unbelief today's reading revealed. Ask God to open your eyes to understanding and believing His Word, and for Him to empower you by His Spirit to obey and walk in the truth.

MEMORY VERSE

Recite or write out each week's memory verse:
Habakkuk 2:14; 1:5; 1:12; 2:4; 2:18.

Group Study Questions

DEFEATING PRIDE: HABAKKUK 2:6-20

- What stood out most to you from this week's lessons? How did it impact you?

- Discuss ways we can feel "plundered" and the promises of God that fill this void.

- Our old sin nature embraces the "insulated" mindset. Has God been revealing insulated tendencies in your own life? If so, what truths have you leaned on to set you free of the lies?

- Across the world and history, inglorious governments wreak havoc. Share practical ways we can live today like Shadrach, Meshach, and Abednego lived in inglorious Babylon—in the world, but not of it.

• Discuss how God's turning Nebuchadnezzar into a mindless grass-eating animal for seven years served as a kindness to him. How does this help us view our trials?

• Jesus is the Great I AM. Idols are the Great I Am Not. What are some of the most popular lies our idols proclaim today? What truths and promises of God can we proclaim to help ourselves and others see the lies and embrace the truth?

• Which attribute of Christ most encouraged you this week?

BREAK UP INTO GROUPS OF TWO OR THREE.

Practice your memory verse with each other, share prayer requests, and then pray for each other.

> What profit is an idol
>   when its maker has shaped it,
>   a metal image, a teacher of lies?
> For its maker trusts in his own creation
>   when he makes speechless idols!

—HABAKKUK 2:18

transforming
fear into
faith

HABAKKUK 3:1–15

TODAY'S READING

Habakkuk 3:1

INTENT

- Habakkuk wrote his prayer as a psalm to be sung for generations.
- **Shigionoth:** Most commentators believe a *Shigionoth* is a type of song that conveys intense feelings through rapid changes of rhythm and emotions, like a victory anthem.

TRUTH

My garden has heard many prayers and praises—and seen many tears. There was a time when it saw more tears than joy, and my prayers sounded like Habakkuk's earlier ones.

I prayed, "O LORD, how long shall I cry for help, and you will not hear? Or cry to you, 'Change me!' and you will not save?"

Pray and study Habakkuk 3:1 in the chart. Note words or phrases that reveal the character, nature, and ways of God and that of anyone or anything else in the passage.

TRUTHS ABOUT GOD	VERSE	TRUTHS ABOUT OTHERS
	[1] A prayer of Habakkuk the prophet, according to Shigionoth.	

Prayer Leads to Praise

Cue the music.

Through the Holy Spirit's inspiration, Habakkuk the prophet directed the appropriate music for his prayer. Don't you wish we had the choirmaster's score and could sing this prayer as the Holy Spirit directed it? We don't have the music, but we have Habakkuk's glorious words.

God commands prayer and uses it to bring about His sovereign will, which He fixed in eternity past. Exactly how prayer works is a mystery—at least to me. But He's called us to pray, so we pray with confidence that God will use our prayers to accomplish His good purposes—which mainly includes changing us. God used Habakkuk's prayers to change him from an anguished prophet to a rejoicing prophet. Let's look at a few aspects of prayer Habakkuk modeled for us.

Humility and Repentance

Habakkuk came boldly to God's throne of grace, as His humble servant rather than a demanding customer. God delights in the prayers of the humble and repentant, but not in attempts to control Him or place demands on Him. Charles Spurgeon said, "While prayer adores God, it lays the creature where he should be—in the very dust."[17] Habakkuk approached God as we should—as the High and Holy One.

Persistence

Habakkuk was quite the persistent pray-er, and his prayers pleased God. To be fair, the Holy Spirit inspired his prayer in the book of Habakkuk. But He'll help us too. He promised (Romans 8:26–27). So let's humbly persist.

Set aside time to pray each day, especially if you don't want to. None of us have enough time, so we must trust God with this challenge.

Martin Luther once said, and it convicts me continually, that his plans for the next day were to "work, work from early till late. In fact I have so much to do that I shall spend the first three hours in prayer."[18]

Honesty

Habakkuk prayed persistently and in humility, but also with raw emotion. He posed honest questions and voiced heartfelt concerns about God's plans.

The Lord already knows every thought we have and emotion we battle. We can't hide anything from Him. He invites us to come as we are with a sincere heart. The Holy Spirit didn't condemn Habakkuk in his weakness, and He won't condemn us. He'll help us (Romans 8:26).

Prayer isn't about the beauty of our words but our honest cry. Let's not be like the hypocrites who love to pray where others will hear them. Jesus said the praise of man will be their only reward (Matthew 6:5). Instead, let's pray honest prayers like Habakkuk.

Surrender

Habakkuk didn't get the answer to his prayer that he wanted. Nevertheless, he surrendered to the answer God gave, even though it terrified him. Like Jesus in the garden of Gethsemane, Habakkuk wanted God's will no matter the cost. Rather than fight the One who knows what's best, is able to provide what's best, and loves us with an everlasting love, let's surrender.

Transformation

Habakkuk didn't change God's mind through his persistent and humble prayers. God changed Habakkuk. God transformed him from complaining and confused "O Lord, how long?" to confident and grateful "I will take joy in the God of my salvation!" He did the same for me. In time, and through much prayer, He transformed me from almost demanding my will and definitely resistant to His to embracing His will and praising Him for it.

What is your biggest struggle with prayer? Ironically, we must go to God in prayer about our struggles with prayer. Pray and ask God to open your eyes to what makes prayer hard for you and seek His divine solutions.

Jesus taught His disciples how to pray in Matthew 6:9–13. Elisabeth Elliot said of this prayer, "I have come to see that it comprises all that really matters in life."[19]

Pray through the Lord's Prayer. Consider adding it to your daily prayer time.

TRANSFORMATION

Jesus is our intercessor. He's at the right hand of God, interceding for us (Romans 8:34). This truth should amaze us. Jesus Christ, our great high priest, the One who is "holy, innocent, unstained, separated from sinners, and exalted above the heavens" is praying for us (Hebrews 7:26). He always lives to make intercession for us (v. 25). May we give prayer the place it deserves in our day and lift our praises to Him for the comfort this truth brings. "Who is to condemn? Christ Jesus is the one who died—more than that, who was raised—who is at the right hand of God, who indeed is interceding for us" (Romans 8:34).

> To say that "prayer changes things" is not as close to the truth as saying, "Prayer changes *me* and then I change things." God has established things so that prayer, on the basis of redemption, changes the way a person looks at things. Prayer is not a matter of changing things externally, but one of working miracles in a person's inner nature.
>
> **OSWALD CHAMBERS,**
> *MY UTMOST FOR HIS HIGHEST*

Prayer doesn't change God's mind.
It changes us and leads to praise.

Consider the truths in today's reading and write a response to the following question.

If I truly believe and act on what God has revealed in this passage, how will the motivations and attitudes of my heart transform and my actions be different tomorrow?

Pray and confess any areas of unbelief today's reading revealed. Ask God to open your eyes to understanding and believing His Word, and for Him to empower you by His Spirit to obey and walk in the truth.

MEMORY VERSE

Read this week's memory verse aloud five times.

O LORD, I have heard the report of you,
　　and your work, O LORD, do I fear.
In the midst of the years revive it;
　　in the midst of the years make it known;
　　in wrath remember mercy.

—HABAKKUK 3:2

TODAY'S READING

Habakkuk 3:2

INTENT

• **Report:** The report Habakkuk heard is the report of what God had decreed against both Judah and Babylon and the report of His great works across eternity as the righteous Judge of all the earth. The report of the whole Bible is the theme of Christ revealed as our righteous creator, redeemer, ruler, and judge.

TRUTH

What comes to your mind when you think about God?

Go ahead, list some thoughts.

_____

_____

_____

As high and lofty as our thoughts may be about the Lord, our fear of Him—our reverence, awe, and adoration tinged with a touch of terror at His blazing holiness—is probably not as high as we think.

How could our earthly thoughts ascend to the heights of His holiness and splendor?

How could earth-dwellers understand the heavenly?

The finite grasp the infinite?

No, our fear of God is most likely not where it should be.

But when we, like Habakkuk, feed our minds with the glorious reports of God in Scripture, God will grow in us a reverent fear of Him and His works and transform our anxious fears into faith.

The more we fear God, the more we'll fear not.

Pray and study the first half of Habakkuk 3:2 in the chart. (We'll look at the second half tomorrow.) Note words or phrases that reveal the character, nature, and ways of God and that of anyone or anything else in the passage.

TRUTHS ABOUT GOD	VERSE	TRUTHS ABOUT OTHERS
	² O Lord, I have heard the report of you, and your work, O Lord, do I fear.	

Knowing versus Fearing

Habakkuk knew and feared God. And rejoiced. Satan knows but doesn't fear God. And is doomed.

Satan knows the truth of who God is. He's witnessed reports Habakkuk only heard or read about in Scripture. But Satan rejects the truth that only in Christ can we find true joy and power. That submission to Jesus delights our souls more than self-exaltation or the praise of man ever could. That outside of God, there's no good thing.

Satan once served God in heaven. He knows more about the Lord than we do. But he doesn't know God like Christians do because God's Spirit doesn't live in Satan. God's Spirit lives in us. Only death, darkness, and lies live in Satan.

Come and hear, all you who fear God, and I will tell what he has done for my soul. (Psalm 66:16)

Habakkuk didn't write this psalm, but it fits perfectly with his psalm. "O Lord, I have heard the report of you, and your work, O Lord, do I fear" (Habakkuk 3:2).

The Holy Spirit inspires growing, not lackluster, faith in God's children. But we all start at ground zero. Seek to know God through His Word and be patient with yourself as you learn, but be diligent.

Fear God and Fear Not

Jesus and His disciples set off in a boat for the other side of the lake. Far from shore, a violent storm sprung up. Waves battered their boat, and terror gripped the seasoned fishermen. But Jesus slept.

Read Mark 4:35–41.

In His humanity, Jesus fell into a deep sleep, exhausted from a full day of ministry. In His divinity, Jesus could sleep in a storm because He always knew His purpose. He came to die on a cross, not in the Sea of Galilee. He'd said, "Let us go across to the other side," not "Let's sink in the middle of the lake." The disciples didn't know about the cross yet and didn't need to. They only needed to know and fear Him.

They had seen Christ feed thousands and heal the sick, but what good was this power if they were all dead?

The disciples woke Jesus and accused Him of not loving them enough. "Teacher, do you not care that we are perishing?"

Jesus stood and rebuked the wind and sea. "Peace! Be still!"

Instantly, the wind ceased, and the waves quieted.

Jesus turned to His disciples. "Why are you so afraid? Have you still no faith?"

Think about the last time anxiety gripped you, then ponder Christ's question to His faithful disciples and ask the same question of yourself. Journal your thoughts.

_____

_____

_____

_____

Terror of the waves had consumed the disciples. But Jesus turned their fear of the sea into awe and fear of the man in the boat. A wondrous fear.

A great calm came over the sea, but the disciples' hearts and minds still churned. Who was this man in the boat with them?

Who was this man who could sleep peacefully while they panicked?

Who could quiet a storm with just a word?

Just a word. Like in the beginning of creation.

"Who then is this, that even the wind and the sea obey him?" (Mark 4:41).

Such a man is not to be trifled with. He is to be feared. And adored. *Fear Me, not your storms.*

Journal your thoughts about the truth that the power of the violent storm on the sea couldn't compare to the power of the man in their boat. Is your fear of Christ greater than your fear of your storms?

_____

_____

_____

_____

Pray through Isaiah 43:1–44:8 and consider Judah, the disciples, and your storms as you pray.

Heard the Reports

A proper fear of God starts at salvation. From there we have much to learn.

Habakkuk revealed that one of the ways God grows our fear of Him is through the reports of Him—God's Word.

"O LORD, I have heard the report of you, and your work, O LORD, do I fear" (Habakkuk 3:2).

When the Lord spoke, Habakkuk listened and believed.

Every complaint Habakkuk held about the soundness of the Lord's plans melted away as God's Word to him renewed his mind, revived his heart, and instilled in him a fresh fear of his God.

Write out Proverbs 9:10.

_____

_____

_____

Write out Romans 12:2.

_____

_____

_____

_____

Apart from an accurate understanding of the Word of God, we can never develop a proper fear of the God of the Word.

Having too low of a view of God and too high of a view of ourselves places us on dangerous ground. In our humanness, we're all guilty of this—like the disciples. They faithfully followed Jesus, but they still didn't truly understand who He is. They still feared the storm more than Jesus. At first. Their view of Him shot high with just three words. "Peace! Be still!"

Consider the depth of your faith today. If you were in the boat with Jesus and the disciples, where would you most likely be? Sleeping next to Jesus or panicking with the disciples?

Wherever our fear of God (our view of Him) rests today, we can be sure it's lower than it will be when we see Him face-to-face. Our understanding of Him is still too small. But we can rejoice because Christ is at work in us. "I am sure of this, that he who began a good work in you will bring it to completion at the day of Jesus Christ" (Philippians 1:6).

We can often have a proper fear of God one minute and then the next, something triggers us to doubt what we firmly believed only a minute before. When I receive a call from one of my children at an unexpected time, anxiety can rise that something must be wrong if they're calling at this time. My view of God's goodness and power shrinks as my fears grow.

Until I remember the three words from the Man in the boat in the storm. "Peace! Be still!"

What circumstances (or people) can trigger your fears and lower your view of the Lord?

"Peace! Be still!"

TRANSFORMATION

Jesus is the lifter of my head. "But you, O Lord, are a shield about me, my glory, and the lifter of my head" (Psalm 3:3). When storms in our world and in our heart cause our gaze to sink toward despair, Christ is the lifter of our head. He is our shield and our glory. He surrounds us with His love and power and lifts our faith to new heights, filling us with courage and joy.

Fear God, and fear not.

Consider the truths in today's reading and write a response to the following question.

If I truly believe and act on what God has revealed in this passage, how will the motivations and attitudes of my heart transform and my actions be different tomorrow?

_____

_____

Pray and confess any areas of unbelief today's reading revealed. Ask God to open your eyes to understanding and believing His Word, and for Him to empower you by His Spirit to obey and walk in the truth.

MEMORY VERSE

Write out this week's memory verse: Habakkuk 3:2.

TODAY'S READING

Habakkuk 3:2

INTENT

- "In the midst of the years" means "in their day."
- "Revive it/make it known" means "Do your mighty works again; make your power known."
- "In wrath remember mercy" means "In your rightful anger over our sin, act mercifully toward us."
- God does not need to be reminded. He never forgets. When the Bible says God "remembers," it means He's setting an action into motion. When the Bible says God "forgets," it means He's choosing not to remember.

TRUTH

How quickly we forget—or at least I do.

My forgetfulness never burned down our house, but I confess that when the smoke alarm sounded, my children ran to the dinner table rather than the nearest exit. "Dinner's ready!" In my defense, the smoke alarm was touchy, and I had more interesting things to do than watch dinner cook . . . or set a timer.

But even this is not as bad as the time I planned a birthday party for my five-year-old son and forgot to invite any guests. I only realized what I'd done when no one came.

Pray and study the second half of Habakkuk 3:2 in the chart. Note words or phrases that reveal the character, nature, and ways of God and that of anyone or anything else in the passage.

TRUTHS ABOUT GOD	VERSE	TRUTHS ABOUT OTHERS
	² In the midst of the years revive it; in the midst of the years make it known; in wrath remember mercy.	

Never Forget to Remember

"Only take care, and keep your soul diligently, lest you forget the things that your eyes have seen, and lest they depart from your heart all the days of your life. Make them known to your children and your children's children" (Deuteronomy 4:9).

No sooner does God say, "Remember," than we say, "Remember what?"

No sooner did God tell Israel, "Have no other gods before me or make any graven images," than Israel crafted a golden calf. Moses's brother Aaron hoisted it into the air and said, "These are your gods, O Israel, who brought you up out of the land of Egypt!" (Exodus 32:8).

I have no words.

No, wait. I do—we are a sinfully forgetful people.

But God is a merciful God. (It's why we sinners are still alive.)

The depth and breadth of Judah's "forgetfulness" is sickeningly stunning. God rescued Israel in great power from Egypt and provided for them for forty years in the wilderness without grocery stores or malls. Their shoes and clothes never wore out. He was their sun and shield. But when they took possession of the land He gave them, they *forgot* they could trust Him.

Read Deuteronomy 4:25–31.

In verse 29 below, circle *but*, *and*, *if*, and *with*, and consider the significance of these words.

> But from there you will seek the LORD your God and you will find him, if you search after him with all your heart and with all your soul.

How does Deuteronomy 4:31 tell us that not all hope was lost for Judah?

Who God Is, Is What God Does

God is incomprehensible. He's the sum of every glorious attribute that radiates from His divine nature, including being wonderfully merciful. Not me. When someone wrongs me, I almost always have to work up mercy in my heart toward them.

The morning as I was writing this lesson, something happened that caused wrath to roar in me like a lion. I had to search every corner of my heart to find mercy. It took me so long to find it, I thought my wrath had eaten mercy for breakfast.

God never has to search for mercy in His heart. Or remember to be merciful. He *is* merciful. He acts mercifully because it's who He is. "For the Lord your God is a merciful God" (Deuteronomy 4:31).

He's also a God of wrath (Romans 1:18). Unlike me, though, His wrath isn't tainted with sin. His wrath burns holy and hot over the destruction sin causes His creation (us) and over the putrid offense sin is to His holiness.

Because God is a God of wrath, He must judge sin.

Because He's a God of mercy, He judged our sin in His Son instead. Jesus willingly took on our sin so He could satisfy God's wrath by His own blood. In wrath, our Lord God remembered mercy.

Who God is, is what God does. He's the Great I AM.

One of Judah's worst sins was turning to idols. We turn to idols because we "forget" who our God is. Write out Psalm 84:11.

_____

_____

What do we lack when we walk with God?

_____

A Better Perspective

Between chapters one and three, Habakkuk changed.

In chapter one, Habakkuk brought his complaints and confusion to God.

In chapter two, God brought Habakkuk clarity and renewed his confidence in God.

In chapter three, Habakkuk's confidence soared and his heart rejoiced.

God had given Habakkuk a better perspective—a proper one. He stepped Habakkuk back from his myopic human view and gave him a more heavenly view. A fuller context in which to interpret what he saw and heard.

His corrected interpretation declared woe to Judah. It was going to be bad. But woe to Babylon even more. It was going to be epic. Like in the days when God delivered Israel from Egypt.

The Lord is the Holy One and the Rock of their salvation. He would judge Babylon, rescue His people, and flood the earth with His glory.

God's Glory above All

In the middle of the five woes, God gave Habakkuk renewed hope and a refreshing break from the carnage when He declared His glory would one day cover the earth.

God's glory is His highest purpose. Not our or Habakkuk's comfort. Definitely not Judah's. They wouldn't know comfort for a long time.

But when we see God's glory—even the smallest glimpse—we enjoy blessings even in our discomfort and our pain.

God's glory never harms His children because there's no condemnation for those in Christ Jesus (Romans 8:1). But that doesn't mean His glory doesn't have teeth at times. It can bring us sharp pain, but it's the faithful pain of a loving Father who disciplines those He loves.

God cares more about our character than our comfort—like He did Judah's and Habakkuk's. When God focused Habakkuk on His glory, God's glory became Habakkuk's greatest desire.

What truly is your greatest desire? Your greatest longing? Take some time to think through these questions.

_____

_____

_____

What would those who know you best say you long for most? What would they write on your tombstone?

_____

_____

In Wrath, God Remembers Mercy

When our oldest daughter was a baby, Larry cradled her in one arm while playing basketball with our three-year-old son. Pretending to be serious, Larry asked Bobby if he should toss Brittany into the basketball goal. Bobby looked dismayed but displayed utter trust in his dad when he said, "Okay, but throw her gently."

This is the kind of faith Habakkuk displayed when he said, "In wrath, remember mercy." Habakkuk knew Judah deserved God's wrath, but the thought of the suffering they'd endure led him to pray in words young Bobby might have prayed, "Okay, God, but throw Judah gently."

What is your biggest struggle today?

_____

_____

Often, our struggle isn't our actual situation, but how to trust God's sovereignty in it. When my mom got cancer, her cancer wasn't my struggle. My accepting God's will for her life was—until I remembered His unfailing character.

Babylon wasn't Habakkuk's struggle. Trusting God's choice to send Babylon was—until he remembered God's mercy.

What's holding you back from trusting God with the same confidence Habakkuk displayed in chapter 3?

TRANSFORMATION

Jesus is the same yesterday and today and forever (Hebrews 13:8). He never changes. "He remains faithful—for he cannot deny himself" (2 Timothy 2:13).

It's in remembering who Christ is that we come to trust what He does. Seek to know Him in every book and every page of the Bible, and let His radiant glory fill you with confidence, peace, and joy.

TRANSFORMATIONAL TRUTH

Who God is, is what God does.

Consider the truths in today's reading and write a response to the following question.

If I truly believe and act on what God has revealed in this passage, how will the motivations and attitudes of my heart transform and my actions be different tomorrow?

_____

_____

Pray and confess any areas of unbelief today's reading revealed. Ask God to open your eyes to understanding and believing His Word, and for Him to empower you by His Spirit to obey and walk in the truth.

MEMORY VERSE

Write out this week's memory verse: Habakkuk 3:2.

TODAY'S READING

Habakkuk 3:3–4

INTENT

- Habakkuk 3:3–15 is a theophany—a visible manifestation of God.
- The Hebrew word Habakkuk uses for God in verse 3 is *'elôha*, an ancient poetic name for God, the creator of Israel.[20]
- Teman and Mount Paran sit opposite each other near Mount Sinai where God came to His chosen people in visible but veiled glory and gave them His law after He brought them out of Egypt (Deuteronomy 33:2).
- Habakkuk used the future tense for the Hebrew word translated as "came" (v. 3). "God shall come" speaks to His coming as progressively unfolding until Christ returns.
- The word *Selah* appears only in the books of Psalms and Habakkuk. Its meaning is uncertain, but some believe it means "to pause and lift your praise."[21]

TRUTH

Larry and I sat on a sand dune after sunset and watched a storm over the South Carolina ocean light the sky. And we prayed. Larry melted my heart as he thanked God for me and devoted our relationship to God's glory. And then he reached into his pocket, pulled out a diamond ring, and asked me to marry him.

Rarely speechless, I blubbered, "Yes!" as he slid the ring onto my finger.

But there was a problem.

The sky was so dark, I couldn't see my ring.

I held it up toward the sky in hopes that the moon might break through the storm clouds and shine onto my ring. But the clouds held back the light. And then, in an instant, lightning flashed. Its blinding light revealed my diamond's glorious radiance.

Pray and study Habakkuk 3:3–4 in the chart. Note words or phrases that reveal the character, nature, and ways of God and that of anyone or anything else in the passage.

TRUTHS ABOUT GOD	VERSE	TRUTHS ABOUT OTHERS
	³ God came from Teman, and the Holy One from Mount Paran. *Selah* His splendor covered the heavens, and the earth was full of his praise.	
	⁴ His brightness was like the light; rays flashed from his hand; and there he veiled his power.	

God Came That You May Know

God came.

He came to Habakkuk to comfort His prophet and proclaim His plans for His rebellious children in Judah. But it was hard for Habakkuk to see any comforting light through the storm clouds of Judah's rebellion and God's fierce judgment. So God turned

Habakkuk's attention to the greatest event in Israel's history thus far. The exodus.

He transported Habakkuk to time in ages past when He came from Teman and Mount Paran. When He came to Mount Sinai in glory and splendor so that they might know and believe in His wisdom and power. That He is the Lord.

The phrase *that you may know* flows throughout the Bible. That you may know.

Not that you may hope or wonder, but that you may know. Remove all your worries and questions and know. What does God want us to know?

Know that God's splendor covers the heavens. Know that the brightness of His glory is like the light. He is the Lord.

Know that He's the same God who came from Teman and Mount Paran. Just as He saved Israel from Egypt in the fullness of time, He'd save Judah from Babylon.

Selah.

When we face a trial, the first information we want to know is if we'll be okay. God gave us 66 books and 1,189 chapters of proof that we'll be okay no matter what—if we belong to Him. He doesn't owe us such an extensive record. He owes us nothing. Journal your thoughts on this.

That We May Know the Way

God's "splendor covered the heavens" (Habakkuk 3:3) when He came in fire on Mount Sinai. Lightning flashed and thunder shook the earth. "I am the LORD your God, who brought you out of the land of Egypt, out of the house of slavery" (Exodus 20:2).

For forty years, God faithfully led His ungrateful and stubborn children through the wilderness in a pillar of clouds by day and fire by night. He dwelled with them in veiled power that they might know the way to go and the way to come to Him—a holy God—and still live despite their sin.

Write out Isaiah 43:10–11.

_____

_____

_____

_____

_____

That We May Know His Glory

Habakkuk described the brightness of the Lord. It "was like the light" (Habakkuk 3:4). "Rays flashed from his hand" (v. 4). Some scholars suggest Habakkuk paints the picture of God holding the stone tablets on which He wrote His law with light from the brightness of His glory shooting out on all sides.

This picture reminds me of Peter, James, and John standing on a different mountain with the Lord as He transfigured before them. On the Mount of Transfiguration, Jesus's face shone like the sun. He stood with Moses and Elijah in radiant splendor. Then a bright cloud overshadowed them, and God spoke from heaven. "This is my beloved Son, with whom I am well pleased; listen to him" (Matthew 17:5).

The disciples could rest in the Lord whose glory shone around them. He would go to the cross in power veiled in flesh, and He would die. But He would rise again in radiant glory on the third day. His power knows no end, and His wisdom is matchless. In His death, He brought forth life.

If you had to describe Christ's power, wisdom, and glory in one sentence, what would you say?

_____

_____

The next time you face a trial, big or small, remember what you wrote and then wrap your mind around this truth—Christ's glory, power, and all that He truly is, is even greater still.

TRANSFORMATION

Jesus is the power and wisdom of God. The Lord's thoughts are not our thoughts, and His ways are not ours either (Isaiah 55:8). They may seem foolish at times, but "the foolishness of God is wiser than men, and the weakness of God is stronger than men" (1 Corinthians 1:25). Consider the cross.

There will always be circumstances we can't understand, but we can know Him, and He is enough. His radiance outshines the sun. His wisdom is beyond understanding. His power knows no limit.

Judah could rest in the God who shone in power on Mount Sinai. In divine wisdom, He would go with them into Babylon and redeem them at the end of the appointed time.

God sends us into trials that we may know Him and His salvation. Though the storm clouds veil His light, in an instant, Christ breaks through in wisdom and power with His salvation. Wait without fear.

He's coming. He came. And He's coming again.
Selah.

Jesus came that we might know Him and His salvation. Trials come for the same reason.

Consider the truths in today's reading and write a response to the following question.

If I truly believe and act on what God has revealed in this passage, how will the motivations and attitudes of my heart transform and my actions be different tomorrow?

Pray and confess any areas of unbelief today's reading revealed. Ask God to open your eyes to understanding and believing His Word, and for Him to empower you by His Spirit to obey and walk in the truth.

MEMORY VERSE

Write out this week's memory verse: Habakkuk 3:2.

day five

TODAY'S READING

Habakkuk 3:5–7

INTENT

- The *him*, *his*, and *he* in verses 5–6 refer to God.
- *Cushan* may refer to the first nation to oppress Israel in the promised land (Judges 3:7–11).
- *Midian* may refer to the events surrounding Gideon in Judges 6–7.

TRUTH

"You keep him in perfect peace whose mind is stayed on you" (Isaiah 26:3).

Sumirnol

Throughout history, God's people couldn't keep their minds stayed on Him. Their sinful desires and worthless idols captured their attention—a lot (Judges 2:10–12). So God shook them up. He turned them over to their enemies. When they cried out to Him, He raised a deliverer.

Pray and study Habakkuk 3:5–7 in the chart. Note words or phrases that reveal the character, nature, and ways of God and that of anyone or anything else in the passage.

TRUTHS ABOUT GOD	VERSE	TRUTHS ABOUT OTHERS
	⁵ Before him went pestilence, and plague followed at his heels.	
	⁶ He stood and measured the earth; he looked and shook the nations; then the eternal mountains were scattered; the everlasting hills sank low. His were the everlasting ways.	
	⁷ I saw the tents of Cushan in affliction; the curtains of the land of Midian did tremble.	

Mighty Warrior

As God prepared to send the nation of Babylon to shake up Judah, He sent Habakkuk down memory lane. He reminded him of when He shook the earth and nations and sent them reeling. How pestilence led the way and plague followed like shield bearers and servants doing the will of their Commander when He delivered Israel from Egypt's power (Deuteronomy 32).

He brought to remembrance Israel's first judge, Othniel, who brought affliction to the tents of Cushan-rishathaim and delivered Israel by God's strong hand (Habakkuk 3:7; Judges 3:7–11). And He pointed to Israel's judge, Gideon. Through weak Gideon, God showed himself strong and made the curtains of Midian tremble (Habakkuk 3:7; Judges 6–7).

Read Judges 6:1–24.

Gideon, God's "mighty warrior," peaked over the edge of the winepress where he secretly threshed his wheat. Had he heard correctly? God had chosen him to save God's people from their enemies? Gideon said to Him, "Please, Lord, how can I save Israel? Behold, my clan is the weakest in Manasseh, and I am the least in my father's house" (v. 15).

Who chooses the least of the weakest to be a deliverer?

The apostle Paul has some thoughts.

Read 2 Corinthians 12:9–10.

Paul delighted in weaknesses, insults, hardships, persecutions, and difficulties. The last I checked none of these words are listed in my gratitude journal. But they should be. "'My grace is sufficient for you, for my power is made perfect in weakness.' . . . For when I am weak, then I am strong" (vv. 9–10).

What are some of your weaknesses? (Add them to your gratitude journal, if you keep one.)

As God reminded Habakkuk, He makes the eternal mountains and everlasting hills bow before Him. He can shatter them and sink them from where they've stood since creation. What is the strength of the Midianites or the weakness of Gideon to God? Unlike Gideon, God was unshakable.

God Shakes Us Up to Build Us Up

God shook His mighty warrior up to take him from where he was (hiding in the winepress) to where he needed to be (ready to lead the battle).

Bit by bit, God worked through His Spirit to build Gideon's weak faith. When Gideon asked for two signs that the Lord *really, really* would help him, God obliged (Judges 6:36–40).

Gideon needed the encouragement because God was about to shake him up more.

God reduced Gideon's army from 32,000 men to 10,000, and finally to a meager 300 men. Three hundred against an armed enemy camped in the valley like a vast swarm of locusts (6:5; 7:1–8).

God then told Gideon, "Arise, go down against the camp, for I have given it into your hand. *But if you are afraid . . .*" (vv. 9–10). Bit by bit, God built up His warrior.

In glorious grace, God meets us in our fears and doubts and carries us to faith.

Read Judges 7:9–15. Write three things Gideon did in verse 15.

_____

_____

While Israel's enemy slept, Gideon and his new mini-sized army carried trumpets and jar-covered torches to the edge of the enemy camp. On command, they blew their trumpets, broke their jars, and shouted, "A sword for the Lord and for Gideon!" (v. 20).

The sound jolted the enemy army out of their sleep and sent them scrambling out of their tents. At the sight of fire flaming across the horizon, the soldiers cried out, fled, and turned their swords against each other.

God shook His enemy and sent them reeling. The curtains of Midian did tremble.

God moves *for*, *in*, and *through* His Children

God's bullet-train ride through history strengthened Habakkuk's confidence that He shakes the earth and nations in power to do a great work *for*, *in*, and *through* His children. He shakes up His children to build up their faith.

- *For* His children to lead them to repentance and a proper fear of Him.
- *In* His children to restore them into His fellowship and strengthen their faith.
- *Through* His children to display His glory and salvation.

Has God been shaking you and your world? If not, hold on. He will. But do not fear. He's doing a great work and building in you a great faith. (But when you do tremble from your hair follicles to your toenails, remember, you can trust Him. And you'll have an amazing story to tell in the end.)

> Those who delight in God's works in the past
> and trust in His promises for the future
> will rest in Him today.
>
> How?
>
> Know the Word.
> Know the Word.
> Know the Word.
> And pray, pray, pray.

Starting this year, if you read through the Bible at least every other year until you're one hundred years old, how many times will you have read through the Bible? _____

TRANSFORMATION

Jesus is our wonderful Counselor, mighty God, everlasting Father, and Prince of Peace. "For to us a child is born, to us a son is given; and the government shall be upon his shoulder, and his name shall be called Wonderful Counselor, Mighty God, Everlasting Father, Prince of Peace" (Isaiah 9:6).

Isaiah prophesied about the birth of Jesus Christ, but few proclaimed His glory when He came. He shook up the wrong people—at least in their opinion He did. But God chose certain men who would believe in Him and the words Isaiah proclaimed about Him. From this group, God built His church and shook the nations with the gospel and raised up more mighty warriors of faith. His grace is sufficient. His power is made perfect in weakness.

TRANSFORMATIONAL TRUTH

God shakes us up to build us up.

Consider the truths in today's reading and write a response to the following question.

If I truly believe and act on what God has revealed in this passage, how will the motivations and attitudes of my heart transform and my actions be different tomorrow?

_____

_____

Pray and confess any areas of unbelief today's reading revealed. Ask God to open your eyes to understanding and believing His Word, and for Him to empower you by His Spirit to obey and walk in the truth.

MEMORY VERSE

Write this week's memory verse and any two from earlier weeks: Habakkuk 2:14; 1:5; 1:12; 2:4; 2:18.

Group Study Questions

TRANSFORMING FEAR INTO FAITH: HABAKKUK 3:1–15

- What stood out most to you from this week's lessons? How did it impact you?

- How did your thoughts on prayer change as you considered how Habakkuk modeled a life of prayer?

- Our view of God tends to seesaw between a high and low view, especially in difficult times. Brainstorm helpful indicators that our view of God is not as high as it should be.

- Were you surprised that God's highest purpose is His glory? Discuss why this is for our good.

- Discuss why, if we believe enough for salvation, we so often fail to believe the truth and stand firm in it in daily life? To believe truth conquers all?

- For fun, add up how many times the whole Bible would be read in your group if you all lived to be one hundred. _____

- Which attribute of Christ most encouraged you this week?

BREAK UP INTO GROUPS OF TWO OR THREE.

Practice your memory verse with each other, share prayer requests, and then pray for each other.

> O Lord, I have heard the report of you,
>   and your work, O Lord, do I fear.
> In the midst of the years revive it;
>   in the midst of the years make it known;
>   in wrath remember mercy.
>
> **—HABAKKUK 3:2**

standing *in* unshakable faith

HABAKKUK 3:16–19

TODAY'S READING

Habakkuk 3 with a view to God's work for His people since eternity past.

INTENT

- Habakkuk switches from talking *about* God to talking *to* God.
- To dramatically display Yahweh's salvation of His people in seemingly impossible circumstances, Habakkuk used rhetorical questions, personification, and anthropomorphism (giving God humanlike features to help us better understand Him and His ways).
- Each of today's verses points us to the exodus from Egypt and into Canaan.
- The poetic images Habakkuk created for God's people to sing throughout all generations weren't analogies or parables. They were history—their history with their God. And their God is our God.

TRUTH

I tried to sabotage my marriage before my wedding day.

Doubt had crept in. Why would Larry choose to marry me? He must not truly know me. Once he did, surely he'd run.

Better he run before the wedding than after, so I set out to prove my rottenness. To show him a different side of me—a shrewish side.

Larry noticed. And didn't run. Instead, he held my face in his hands and said, "You're beautiful."

I married him.

Pray and study Habakkuk 3:8–11 in the chart. Note words or phrases that reveal the character, nature, and ways of God and that of anyone or anything else in the passage.

TRUTHS ABOUT GOD	VERSE	TRUTHS ABOUT OTHERS
	⁸ Was your wrath against the rivers, O Lord [Yahweh]? Was your anger against the rivers, or your indignation against the sea, when you rode on your horses, on your chariot of salvation?	
	⁹ You stripped the sheath from your bow, calling for many arrows. *Selah* You split the earth with rivers.	
	¹⁰ The mountains saw you and writhed; the raging waters swept on; the deep gave forth its voice; it lifted its hands on high.	
	¹¹ The sun and moon stood still in their place at the light of your arrows as they sped, at the flash of your glittering spear.	

Unworthy but Loved

Yahweh reminded Habakkuk how He rode out to save His bride from slavery, but not because she's worthy. Because He loves her.

He split the Red Sea into great walls of water (Exodus 14:21–22) and stopped up the Jordan (Joshua 3). He brandished His bow and commanded His arrows against His enemies in the defense of His people.

His glory caused the mountains to quake and the waters to obey and lift their waves in praise and submission to their almighty Creator and King.

He caused the sun and moon to stand still and threw hailstones like lightning to crush those who wanted to crush Israel (10:1–13).

No enemy or force can touch Christ's bride without His permission.

Stop and think about our mighty Savior saving His unfaithful people—and unfaithful us. Like Judah, we are unworthy but loved.

Yahweh knew every unfaithful choice we'd make before He created us—created Judah—and still He made us and placed His love on us forever. Even when He knew we'd be His enemies (Romans 5:10). And yet He loves us with steadfast and unchanging love.

Because of what God did for Israel in the exodus, Habakkuk and Judah could ride out their years in Babylon confident that God would come and save them.

Commit to daily reminding yourself of God's great works. Start now by writing down one past work of God that reminds you of His power, love, or commitment to His bride.

_____

_____

_____

_____

God Defines Love and Salvation

Truth be told, we want to be the ones who define what love and salvation look like. For me, it's freedom from all suffering. It's God forbidding pain to touch me or my loved ones.

I'm not far off. Because Christ suffered and died for me and saved me, when He returns, pain and suffering will never touch me again or my loved ones who've trusted in Him. But that day is not today.

Christ is the definition of love and salvation. He suffered to open the way for all who will believe to find redemption. Our suffering is often the way we finally see our need for Christ.

After salvation, it's often the way we learn the richest truths about Him—and learn to trust Him. We want to know these rich truths. They bring us the joy we hunger for because they lead us into a fuller dependence on Christ our Savior.

Judah needed to remember that the God of salvation who loved and saved them in Egypt is the God who loves them and will come for them in Babylon. Judah was faithless and preferred other gods. Sin carries consequences we must bear for its appointed time (like seventy years in Babylon), but God is here.

He rides His horses on chariots of salvation with His bow raised to deliver His beloved bride.

He bends the will of nature and forces all elements to obey His commands to bring us salvation.

If you're a Christian, begin writing your salvation testimony, but stop after the first five words.

Did you start your testimony by talking about yourself? Salvation doesn't start with us reaching up to God. It starts with God reaching down to us. (No one seeks after God—Romans 3:11.) Rewrite the five words of your testimony starting with *God*.

If you're not a Christian, today's the perfect day to trust in Christ.

Settle It in Your Heart—God Loves You

In college, I was in an almost four-year dating drought. By my senior year, when many of my friends squealed and waved their engagement rings around, I crawled deeper into my "you're such a loser" hole.

I was convinced God had His favorites, and I wasn't one of them. I didn't blame Him. I wasn't my favorite either. But I despaired. And complained to God. It was like me standing at the foot of the cross, watching Jesus suffer and die for me, and saying, "Jesus, why don't you love me enough to give me a husband?"

After I got a husband, I didn't get a job that paid well. I felt overlooked by God.

When I quit my job to raise our children, my husband worked excruciatingly long hours. I felt abandoned by God.

Years later, my mentor, Grace, described the agony Christ endured on the cross for us. As she spoke, I could almost feel the nails and smell His blood as it ran down His hands, His feet, and His sides.

When she finished, she said with steel in her eyes, "Settle it *forever* in your heart that God loves you."

Settle it forever.

I did. I finally did.

Habakkuk settled it forever in his heart that God loves His people. The past works of God to save His bride stood before him as irrefutable evidence of His unfailing love. And Habakkuk didn't even have the cross as proof.

What circumstances have led you to ask Christ why He doesn't love you enough to _____?

TRANSFORMATION

Jesus is love. "Greater love has no one than this, that someone lay down his life for his friends" (John 15:13). Jesus chose to save us because He is love. It's who He is. "God is love" (1 John 4:8).

"For one will scarcely die for a righteous person—though perhaps for a good person one would dare even to die—but God shows his love for us in that while we were still sinners, Christ died for us" (Romans 5:7–8).

All those years ago, I marveled that Larry would choose me. He's continued to choose me every day since. I marvel even more that Christ, our sinless Savior, our Yahweh Elohim—who doesn't need us—chose us. He settled it forever on the cross.

Settle it forever in your heart—God loves you.

Consider the truths in today's reading and write a response to the following question.

If I truly believe and act on what God has revealed in this passage, how will the motivations and attitudes of my heart transform and my actions be different tomorrow?

_____

_____

Pray and confess any areas of unbelief today's reading revealed. Ask God to open your eyes to understanding and believing His Word, and for Him to empower you by His Spirit to obey and walk in the truth.

MEMORY VERSE

Recite this week's memory verses aloud five times.

Though the fig tree should not blossom,
nor fruit be on the vines,
the produce of the olive fail
and the fields yield no food,
the flock be cut off from the fold
and there be no herd in the stalls,
yet I will rejoice in the LORD;
I will take joy in the God of my salvation.

—HABAKKUK 3:17-18

TODAY'S READING

Habakkuk 3 with a view to the future when Christ returns for His beloved bride and sets up His eternal kingdom.

INTENT

- Today's reading continues to display God's salvation of His people in the past as well as in Habakkuk's nearer future (seventy years) and in the end times when Christ returns.
- In verse 13, the Hebrew word for "salvation" is the root word of *Yeshuah*, another Hebrew name for Jesus.
- The Hebrew word for "anointed" can also be translated as *messiah*.
- God called Cyrus, the king of Persia, "his anointed" (Isaiah 45:1). At the end of the Babylonian exile, Cyrus laid the king of Babylon "bare from thigh to neck" (Habakkuk 3:13). Or as one commentary explains, Cyrus destroyed the house (the dynasty) of Babylon in one blow from its gable to its foundation.[22]
- God's ultimate Anointed One is Jesus Christ, our Messiah and Savior. He bruised Satan's head on the cross and will one day deliver the final death blow.

TRUTH

More than 250 years before Habakkuk cried out to God, three fierce armies banded together to destroy Judah. Before the battle, the enemy armies slept peacefully, confident in their odds of three against one. Meanwhile, in Jerusalem, sleep surely evaded Judah's king, Jehoshaphat. He cried out to the Lord of hosts and received a surprising answer (2 Chronicles 20).

God pointed to Judah's past to lift Habakkuk's (and Judah's) hope for their future.

Pray and study Habakkuk 3:12–15 in the chart. Note words or phrases that reveal the character, nature, and ways of God and that of anyone or anything else in the passage.

TRUTHS ABOUT GOD	VERSE	TRUTHS ABOUT OTHERS
	¹² You [Yahweh] marched through the earth in fury; you threshed the nations in anger.	
	¹³ You went out for the salvation of your people, for the salvation of your anointed. You crushed the head of the house of the wicked, laying him bare from thigh to neck. *Selah*	
	¹⁴ You pierced with his own arrows the heads of his warriors, who came like a whirlwind to scatter me, rejoicing as if to devour the poor in secret.	
	¹⁵ You trampled the sea with your horses, the surging of mighty waters.	

Set Your Face

When the armies from Ammon, Moab, and Mount Seir came out to battle Judah, fear gripped King Jehoshaphat. But rather than run to mightier nations for help, Jehoshaphat "set his face to seek the LORD" (2 Chronicles 20:3).

All of Judah followed their king's example and "assembled to seek help from the Lord" (v. 4). As Jehoshaphat stood before God's people, he prayed and proclaimed God's greatness. "O Lord, God of our fathers, are you not God in heaven? You rule over all the kingdoms of the nations. In your hand are power and might, so that none is able to withstand you" (v. 6).

Jehoshaphat then declared God's mighty works on behalf of His people in ages past and ended his prayer with honest humility. "We are powerless against this great horde that is coming against us. We do not know what to do, but our eyes are on you" (v. 12).

Is "a great horde" coming against you? What area of your life do you feel powerless and unsure what to do?

Read God's response to Jehoshaphat through His prophet Jahaziel:

Thus says the LORD to you, "Do not be afraid and do not be dismayed at this great horde, for the battle is not yours but God's. . . . You will not need to fight in this battle. Stand firm, hold your position, and see the salvation of the LORD on your behalf, O Judah and Jerusalem." Do not be afraid and do not be dismayed. Tomorrow go out against them, and the LORD will be with you. (2 Chronicles 20:15, 17)

Who does your battle belong to?

In verses 15 and 17 above, underline what God told Judah to do. Circle what He told them not to do.

In today's reading from Habakkuk, circle in each verse who did all the work of salvation.

Praise Is a Mighty Weapon

When Judah marched out to meet the three armies, a different group of warriors led them into battle. God didn't clothe them in heavy armor and coats of chain mail. He girded them in spiritual armor like the soldier in Ephesians 6:10–18.

God commanded Judah's army to appoint men dressed in holy attire to go before them and sing a song of praise—one line of pure praise and truth.

"Give thanks to the LORD, for his steadfast love endures forever" (2 Chronicles 20:21).

As you face your trials, what type of song rises from your lips? "Nobody knows the trouble I've seen"? Or "Give thanks to the Lord, for his steadfast love endures forever"?

_____

If your heart sings a praise song, do you sing it like a victory anthem or, as I do at times, more like a funeral dirge?

_____

Why do you think God called Judah's army to praise Him before He saved them from destruction rather than waiting until after their enemies' demise?

_____

_____

God Will Be God

The moment the men of Judah began to sing, God moved in power against the Ammonite, Moabite, and Meunite armies. To borrow from Habakkuk, God pierced the heads of the warriors with their own arrows. The Ammonites and Moabites allied together and wiped out the Meunites. Then they turned on each other until no one was left alive. By the time Judah reached the battlefield, all three armies lie dead.

Imagine the shock—and then the thrill—when Judah arrived to find the battle already over. Nothing but carnage and valuable plunder lie before them. It took them three days to gather all the treasure.

God will be God.

As valuable as the plunder was that day, the greatest treasure Judah received was the knowledge and belief that the Lord of hosts is with them wherever they go.

God is the same yesterday, today, and forever. When He declares the future, it's already established as sure as the past. All that John saw and recorded in the book of Revelation is as sure as if it's already happened.

Christ is coming again, and our salvation will reach its final fulfillment in His eternal kingdom. We'll never need saving again. Until then, never forget that God will always be God. His love endures forever (Psalm 136).

At times it feels like God is inching us toward the day when Christ will establish His kingdom and save us from all evil, but He moves at His wise pace. No one can force God's hand or His timing. I'm glad, because if we could, who's to say who gets to manipulate Him? What if two prayers oppose each other? The farmer needs rain for his crops, but the builder can't work in the rain. I don't want your prayers negating mine.

Neither nature nor nations can stop or force His hand. Whether He spares us or, in perfect wisdom, ordains us to endure severe and prolonged trials, the Lord of hosts is with us.

Read Psalm 46. Like Habakkuk 3, Psalm 46 was meant to be sung. Cue the music and praise.

Even if God strips you down to nothing like He did Judah in Habakkuk's days, how prepared do you feel to stand firm in your faith? Is it enough to know that the Lord of hosts is with you? Journal your thoughts.

_____

_____

_____

_____

_____

_____

_____

TRANSFORMATION

Jesus is the Lord of hosts. "The LORD of hosts is with us; the God of Jacob is our fortress. _Selah_" (Psalm 46:11).

God has promised eternal riches that far exceed anything this world can give, but while we live in this world, He calls us to face hard times. Israel faced Pharaoh, Jehoshaphat faced three armies, and Christ faced the cross. But God will never abandon us. The Lord of hosts who's with us is the same God who trampled the sea, pierced the heads of the warriors with their own arrows, and raised Christ from the dead for our salvation.

Neither nations nor nature will stop Him from fulfilling His good purposes for you. Even if the earth were to give way and the mountains be moved into the heart of the sea, the Lord of hosts is with us.

Settle it forever in your heart. God will be God, and He loves you. His loving devotion endures forever.

Selah.

Neither nations nor nature can stop the God of our salvation. God will be God.

Consider the truths in today's reading and write a response to the following question.

If I truly believe and act on what God has revealed in this passage, how will the motivations and attitudes of my heart transform and my actions be different tomorrow?

_____

_____

Pray and confess any areas of unbelief today's reading revealed. Ask God to open your eyes to understanding and believing His Word, and for Him to empower you by His Spirit to obey and walk in the truth.

MEMORY VERSE

Write out this week's memory verses: Habakkuk 3:17–18.

TODAY'S READING

Habakkuk 3 with a view to God's anger toward sin and Satan. Remember how our Redeemer God came with salvation in His Son—and He's coming again to destroy sin, Satan, and death forever.

INTENT

• Habakkuk's theophanies are over. Now he responds in Habakkuk 3:16–19 to what God has shown him.

TRUTH

Ever heard this preschool song? "I'm in-right, outright, upright, downright happy all the time. . . . since Jesus Christ came in and cleansed my heart from sin."

Are you happy all the time?

I'm not. And neither was Habakkuk.

(Joy and happiness aren't the same. Happiness is based on external circumstances. It's fleeting. Joy is internal and based on our unchanging Lord.)

At God's report of Babylon, Habakkuk felt like "rottenness" had entered his bones. (That's not happy.) As Christians we might feel *unspiritual* if we tremble and cry in the face of trials, but Habakkuk didn't. He admitted it.

We're flesh and bone—and flesh and bone feel pain. Pain often brings his buddies angst and anger. This trio can make us emphatically unhappy.

Pray and study Habakkuk 3:16 in the chart. Note words or phrases that reveal the character, nature, and ways of God and that of anyone or anything else in the passage.

TRUTHS ABOUT GOD	VERSE	TRUTHS ABOUT OTHERS
	[16] I hear, and my body trembles; my lips quiver at the sound; rottenness enters into my bones; my legs tremble beneath me. Yet I will quietly wait for the day of trouble to come upon people who invade us.	

Submit Your Emotions to Truth

God is our Rock, but He's not an emotionless rock. And He's endowed us with emotions like His—emotions like love, joy, anger, and sorrow. Sin endowed us with a few God doesn't experience like angst and selfish pride. Habakkuk felt them all.

God's emotions are holy. Ours are stained by sin.

God bolstered Habakkuk's faith with truth and reminders of who He is, but the prophet's flesh and bones still agonized over the coming pain. His legs still trembled. His lips could barely form the words, "Babylon is coming."

Yet Habakkuk had hope. Not for reprieve but for rest.

What makes your lips quiver? Knowing why we're afraid helps us submit all our fears to Christ and find rest for our soul.

The Righteous Find Rest

Noah's name means "rest," but, like Habakkuk, he spent much of his life in unrest. The heart of every man was intent on "only evil continually" (Genesis 6:5). Only Noah was holy. God told him to build an ark to prepare for a judgment even more destructive than a warrior nation—a worldwide flood.

Noah preached for the people to turn from their sin and turn to God. But when the flood came, the people refused to enter into God's rest because of their unbelief. Only eight people—Noah and his family—entered the ark.

Surely Noah wept tears of sorrow. So much loss and death. But I imagine, mingled with his sorrow, flowed grateful tears of joy. He and his family were safe. No matter how fierce the storm raged outside, they enjoyed rest (and life) in the ark.

Soul rest is only found in Christ. No outward storm can touch the soul hidden with Christ (Colossians 3:3). Waters of affliction will churn around us until Christ calls us home or He returns, but we can wait quietly in the day of trouble. We are safe in Him. The Lord of hosts is with us.

> Don't take the pressure of forethought upon yourself. It is not only wrong to worry, it is infidelity, because worrying means that we do not think that God can look after the practical details of our lives, and it is never anything else that worries us.
>
> **OSWALD CHAMBERS,** *MY UTMOST FOR HIS HIGHEST*

Pray through Matthew 6:25, remembering Israel in the wilderness and Noah in the ark.

With God, the Impossible Isn't Difficult—It's Done

Before God brought Israel out of Egypt and into their rest in the promised land, He told them to paint the blood of a lamb on the sides and top of their door. Inside, they were to eat the Passover meal and be ready to leave Egypt. To quietly wait for the moment of trouble to come upon the people who'd enslaved them.

At midnight, the angel of death would pass over each home. If he saw the blood of the lamb, the firstborn son would live. If he didn't, the firstborn son would die.

God never mentioned what kind of emotions He required while they waited. Let's imagine what transpired in three homes.

Inside Impossible Ida's home, Ida clung to their firstborn son and peppered her husband with questions. "How can you eat at a time like this? Don't you care about our son? I don't see how you can believe the blood of a lamb will protect Junior from a death angel." Ida wanted to share her husband's unshakeable faith in God's promise, but her fears made it impossible.

Inside Difficult Donna's home, she nibbled at the food on her plate and held her son close. "Do you feel all right, Junior? Eat up. God is leading us out of here tomorrow. Are you sure you feel alright? Of course, you're fine. God is faithful." She forced a smile. Donna believed but trembled in her belief.

Inside Done Dora's home, laughter rang through the air as they ate the Passover meal. When Junior trembled, Done Dora said, "You're fine, son. The death angel won't touch you. The blood will protect you. Now, pass the bitter herbs." Dora's faith settled the matter in her mind. God's salvation had come. It was as good as done.

With God, the impossible isn't difficult. It's done.

To be clear, the Passover was a serious event. The lamb had to die so their son would not. The point of my illustration is that the level of the people's trembling didn't determine their salvation. It didn't matter if their hands shook as they applied the blood. Their obedience revealed their faith, even if their mustard seed–sized faith trembled (Matthew 17:20).

Those who trusted God's word applied the blood. Those who didn't ignored Him and His salvation. Trembling faith is still saving faith if it's true faith, and true faith brings soul rest.

Habakkuk's trembling revealed his humanity. Fear is a reasonable response to cruel warriors. His obedience revealed his faith. Habakkuk would surrender to the Lord's will, quietly wait for Babylon to arrive, and rejoice in the God of his salvation.

Until Christ returns, our knees will wobble at times, but if we keep our minds fixed on Christ, they'll wobble less, and our hearts will find rest in Yahweh Elohim. No matter how impossible a situation seems or how difficult circumstances become, everything God promises is good—and as good as done.

Behold, I am the LORD, the God of all flesh. Is anything too hard for me? (Jeremiah 32:27)

Which home best describes your faith in a trial? Impossible Ida's unbelief, Difficult Donna's trembling faith, or Done Dora's confident faith?

_____

What are you waiting for before your heart can rejoice? The world to change? Your relationships to improve?

_____

Write out Psalm 46:10.

_____

_____

Write out Isaiah 26:3.

_____

_____

Place a dot on the scale for how peaceful your heart is now. Put an X on how peaceful you've felt this past month.

UTTERLY RATTLED	WOBBLY	PURELY PEACEFUL
●·········●·········●		
0	5	10

TRANSFORMATION

Jesus was a Man of Sorrows (Isaiah 53:3). Jesus sympathizes with our weaknesses (Hebrews 4:15–16). Though we may tremble in our trials like Habakkuk, we can rest and quietly wait on the day when the Man of Sorrows will remove all pain and death because He's accomplished the impossible for us. We can rest because it's done. Christ has opened the way of salvation from sin, sorrow, and all our fears.

TRANSFORMATIONAL TRUTH

With God, the impossible isn't difficult. It's done.

Consider the truths in today's reading and write a response to the following question.

If I truly believe and act on what God has revealed in this passage, how will the motivations and attitudes of my heart transform and my actions be different tomorrow?

_____

_____

Pray and confess any areas of unbelief today's reading revealed. Ask God to open your eyes to understanding and believing His Word, and for Him to empower you by His Spirit to obey and walk in the truth.

MEMORY VERSE

Write out this week's memory verses: Habakkuk 3:17–18.

TODAY'S READING

Habakkuk 3 with God's eternal power and unchanging character in view.

INTENT

• The context within the passage and the verb form of the Hebrew words for *rejoice* and *take joy* both suggest Habakkuk didn't merely accept their fate in Babylon. He embraced joy in the Lord with delight and excitement.[23]

• Habakkuk listed actual—not symbolic—losses Judah would suffer.

TRUTH

The sun had set on all the disciples' hopes and dreams. Jesus was gone.

Imagine what the evening of Christ's death might have been like for the disciples as confusion, fear, and despair gripped them.

Jesus had entrusted His mother to John. Did John long to carry her far away to escape the sights and sounds that would remind them of the evil done to Jesus? *Couldn't Jesus have stopped them? He's the Christ. At least I thought He was.*

What about Peter? Did he lay in the dark, replaying the past twenty-four hours in his tormented mind? Did his bold profession of allegiance mock him? *I'll die for You, Jesus.* Did his abject denial plague him? *I do not know Him.* Surely the memory of Jesus's piercing gaze after the rooster crowed felt like rottenness entering his bones.

Could any of Jesus's disciples sleep that night?

They'd left everything to follow Him.

And now He was gone.

All was gone.

Pray and study Habakkuk 3:17–18 in the chart. Note words or phrases that reveal the character, nature, and ways of God and that of anyone or anything else in the passage.

TRUTHS ABOUT GOD	VERSE	TRUTHS ABOUT OTHERS
	¹⁷ Though the fig tree should not blossom, nor fruit be on the vines, the produce of the olive fail and the fields yield no food, the flock be cut off from the fold and there be no herd in the stalls,	
	¹⁸ yet I will rejoice in the LORD [Yahweh]; I will take joy in the God [Elohim] of my salvation.	

Though All Is Gone, God Remains

Habakkuk and Judah faced the loss of everything. The real and devastating loss of their home and possessions. Some would even lose their lives and the lives of loved ones. But the disciples faced the loss of more if Christ were truly dead and gone forever. All hope would be lost because God's promises would have failed—and God would have ceased to be God.

But God's promises cannot fail.

Christ rose from the dead, just like He promised.

The disciples didn't understand what happened at the cross. It made no sense.

When nothing makes sense, and the sun sets on your hope, step back and look at your situation in the context of our risen Christ.

Though all is gone, God remains.

Let your heart rejoice.

> He [Habakkuk] resolves to delight and triumph in God notwithstanding; when all is gone his God is not gone.
>
> **MATTHEW HENRY,** *MATTHEW HENRY'S COMMENTARY ON THE WHOLE BIBLE*

Struggles Lead to Joy

For most of my life, when I faced a trial, I determined to go around it, ignore it, or at worst keep my head down and slog through it. But one day it struck me that if God in His sovereignty leads me to a struggle, the struggle must be the point.

Our trials aren't random acts of torment that God later redeems by eventually finding some way He can use it for good.

Our struggles don't detour us off the path of joy. They lead us to joy.

That's not to say we should go looking for trouble. Trials will find us (John 16:33). When they come, fear not, and remember that the path to joy leads through the trouble—not around it.

Read James 1:2–4.

When exactly does James tell us to count it all joy?

James sounds like he expects us to meet a lion in the wilderness and shout, "Yippee!" But not even a lion can change the truth. We can trust our powerful God in every situation. This calls for a "Yippee!" and "Amen!"

In the past, I waited to count it all joy until after the trial—after I'd had time to think of some reason to be thankful for my trial. But James says we already have the reason: "*for you know* that the testing of your faith produces steadfastness" (v. 3).

The testing of what we truly believe produces faith as rare and beautiful as diamonds.

Write out why James says we're to let steadfastness have its full effect rather than run from the pressure.

_____

_____

It takes both time and pressure to transform lumps of coal into diamonds—and our faith into priceless gems. God was handing Judah a diamond-producing moment on the path to joy. They would not die. Instead, they would become steadfast, perfect, and complete, lacking nothing.

List three ways James 1:2–4 will impact your decisions if you believe it.

_____

_____

I Will Exult

From Habakkuk's humbled position before the high and holy God, he didn't merely choose to put on a happy face. He rejoiced with delight in the Lord and jumped for holy joy because of one glorious truth: Though all is gone, God remains.

It may seem callous to talk about jumping for joy in the face of destruction. It may even seem absurd or immature. "The natural person does not accept the things of the Spirit of God, for they are folly to him, and he is not able to understand them because they are spiritually discerned" (1 Corinthians 2:14).

Exulting in God's plans even when they call for suffering isn't callous, absurd, or foolish. It's the consequence of joy in the Lord. Of treasuring the Lord above all so that when all else is gone, our joy isn't spoiled.

> Those who, when full, enjoyed God in all, when emptied and poor, can enjoy all in God.
>
> **MATTHEW HENRY,** _MATTHEW HENRY'S COMMENTARY ON THE WHOLE BIBLE_

God Knows What You Need

"But seek first the kingdom of God and his righteousness, and all these things will be added to you" (Matthew 6:33).

James tells us that we don't have because we don't ask, and when we do ask, we ask from selfish reasons (James 4:2–3). Matthew tells us not to worry about what we need. God knows and will provide (Matthew 6:25–34). In other words, "Delight yourself in the LORD, and he will give you the desires of your heart" (Psalm 37:4). Even if you don't ask.

Read Luke 11:1–14.

Notice that "asking" is a primary focus. With this context in mind, what stands out about the man Jesus healed in verse 14? What could he not do?

For thirteen verses, various people asked Jesus to provide. Then in verse 14, Jesus healed a man who didn't (and couldn't) ask for anything—not even his healing. This is the good Father that Matthew, James, and Habakkuk worshipped. The God of salvation who made Habakkuk leap for joy.

How willing are you to trust God to know what you need?

How would your answer change if God says what you need is a struggle—or the struggle you're already in?

_____

_____

_____

Babylons will come into our lives and take our figs, vines, cattle, and herd. And it will be hard. But when all is gone, God remains. He is more than enough. His salvation is coming like the dawn.

TRANSFORMATION

Jesus is the Dawn. "Because of our God's merciful compassion, the Dawn from on high will visit us to shine on those who live in darkness and the shadow of death, to guide our feet into the way of peace" (Luke 1:78–79 HCSB). Where there is the peace of Christ, we will find the joy of our Lord.

The sun had set on all the disciples' hopes and dreams. Jesus was gone. Or so they thought. On the third day, the Dawn from on high rose from the dead—and lives forevermore.

No matter how dark the world becomes in its lust for evil, Christ rises in our souls like the dawn, and the darkness cannot overcome Him. Rejoice!

Though all is gone, God remains. Rejoice!

Consider the truths in today's reading and write a response to the following question.

If I truly believe and act on what God has revealed in this passage, how will I be changed? How will the motivations and attitudes of my heart transform and my actions be different tomorrow?

Pray and confess any areas of unbelief today's reading revealed. Ask God to open your eyes to understanding and believing His Word, and for Him to empower you by His Spirit to obey and walk in the truth.

MEMORY VERSE

Write out this week's memory verses: Habakkuk 3:17–18.

TODAY'S READING

Revelation 21 with a view toward Habakkuk. As you read, notice what part God plays in establishing the new heaven and new earth, and what part man plays. Notice who does what.

INTENT

- Habakkuk uses God's title *Adonai*, which speaks to His right to rule as Lord and Master.
- Habakkuk's audience would have understood that to "tread on my high places" referred to "the victorious possession and government of a land."[24] Reaching the pinnacle, safe and secure.

TRUTH

"How long, O LORD?"
Habakkuk opened with an anguished prayer.
Judah is out of control.

God's answer made the prophet stagger.
Can we talk about this?

And they did.
God talked. Habakkuk listened. And transformed.
God's words stamped an exclamation point over Habakkuk's questions, filled him with strength, and lifted his soul from despair to praise.

Pray and study Habakkuk 3:19 in the chart. Note words or phrases that reveal the character, nature, and ways of God and that of anyone or anything else in the passage.

TRUTHS ABOUT GOD	VERSE	TRUTHS ABOUT OTHERS
	¹⁹ GOD [Yahweh], the Lord [Adonai], is my strength; he makes my feet like the deer's; he makes me tread on my high places. To the choirmaster: with stringed instruments.	

Secure in Holy Joy

The more God spoke, the more Habakkuk found his feet secured in holy joy. His heart, soul, mind, and strength reached the pinnacle of praise as he surrendered his will fully to God as Adonai—his Lord, Master, and supreme authority.

Rather than wrestle against God's authority over his life, he rejoiced that Yahweh Adonai was his God, the King of Kings and the Lord of Lords. Habakkuk delighted to submit to His loving and wise rule.

Pray and ask God to reveal any areas of resistance in your heart to His rule over you and to give you a heart that delights to submit to Him. And then obey with joy.

The Power of *Is*

Every word of Scripture matters, including the tiny word *is* in Habakkuk 3:19. "Yahweh, Adonai, is my strength."

He *is* my strength.

Not only is the Lord my strength, but also His strength is mine. This is two sides of the same coin that promises all the power we need to follow Christ wherever He goes. He is my strength, and all the strength He has is mine.

Nothing is too steep or too high—or too low—unless it is too steep, too high, or too low for the Lord. We know that's not possible.

Consider characters in a video game. We're their strength. They're powerless to move or direct their steps apart from us. I'm terrible at video games, so my avatar always loses. But in the hands of the most skilled player, the same character would always win.

The Lord is my strength, and His strength is mine.

Read Hebrews 13:20–21.

Write down the titles and descriptors listed for God and Jesus.

_____

_____

Note what God does and what we do in this passage. Journal how this fills you with strength.

_____

_____

It's not wrong to ask God for strength, but at least for the next week, don't ask God for strength. Ask Him to remind you that He *is* your strength.

Then walk in it.

Don't wait until you feel strong and sufficient to a challenge. Go in Christ's unfailing strength and joy.

Christ Sets Us in Our High Places

When Habakkuk wrote today's verse, I wonder if the Holy Spirit reminded him of the times King Saul sought to kill David. Saul didn't fail to kill David because David was that clever. He failed because God made David's feet like a deer's, which bound with grace through thickets that would trip and face-plant us. Some deer can even scale the face of a wall.

I watched footage of a doe leading her baby up the steep wall of a dam. Her fawn traipsed after her as if leaping up a stairwell, not onto hoof-holds more suitable for flies than four-legged mammals. A mother deer can lead her baby, but she can't make her fawn's footing secure. Habakkuk reminds us God does it all. He both leads us and makes our feet secure.

This doesn't mean we'll always enjoy worldly success and a life of health and riches. It means we'll enjoy God's pleasure, and joy will fill our souls.

King David spent years living in caves running from Saul. Not exactly the life you'd expect of God's anointed. But David wrote of the Lord, "He made my feet like the feet of a deer and set me secure on the heights" (Psalm 18:33).

In His perfect timing, God made David victorious over all his enemies and set him secure on the throne as ruler over all Israel— every city, hill, and mountain. "And your house and your kingdom shall be made sure forever before me. Your throne shall be established forever" (2 Samuel 7:16). This promise endured through Jesus, the Son of David.

Habakkuk understood and rejoiced. We will not die.

What path is God leading you on that seems filled with microscopic footholds? Pray and ask God to remind you each step that He will hold you secure. Then follow Him without fear. He's making you into a reflection of His Son and leading you into His eternal presence.

Christ Makes Our Steps Light

Whether you're living in high places or low, life on earth is hard, and hard is wearying. Physical, mental, and emotional fatigue make our feet heavy. Fatigue invites doubt to whisper that we cannot go on. But joy in the Lord lifts our weary hearts . . . and our hands and feet. Even if we don't like the path we're on—sickness, sorrow, exhaustion—Christ's strength at work in us makes our steps light.

Hudson Taylor, a fifty-one-year missionary to China in the 1800s, echoed Habakkuk's faith when he said, "It makes no matter where He places me, or how. That is rather for Him to consider than for me, for in the easiest position He must give me His grace, and in the most difficult His grace is sufficient."[25]

Though Babylon was coming, Habakkuk knew God, not man, determined his steps. He knew God would bring them through the fire of Babylon, shining like refined silver and gold. This truth lightened his steps and his heart.

Can you think of a time when the joy of the Lord made something heavy feel lighter? Journal about your experience. If you can't remember a time, journal a prayer, asking God to help you understand and believe that His joy is your never-failing strength.

_____

_____

_____

_____

_____

_____

TRANSFORMATION

Jesus is our strength and our song (Psalm 118:14). His strength makes our feet like the deer's, able to walk with holy joy, even in our steepest trials and deepest fears. Our Adonai lifts the souls of those who trust in Him and sets us securely in Him.

> The LORD is my strength and my song;
>   he has become my salvation.
> Glad songs of salvation
>   are in the tents of the righteous:
> "The right hand of the LORD does valiantly,
>   the right hand of the LORD exalts,
>   the right hand of the LORD does valiantly!"
> I shall not die, but I shall live,
>   and recount the deeds of the LORD.

> **—PSALM 118:14–17**

Selah.

TRANSFORMATIONAL TRUTH

The Lord is my strength, and His strength is mine.

We've come to the end of the book of Habakkuk. Can you believe it? Consider the truths in today's reading and write a response to the following question.

> *If I truly believe and act on what God has revealed in this passage, how will the motivations and attitudes of my heart transform and my actions be different tomorrow?*

Pray and confess any areas of unbelief today's reading revealed. Ask God to open your eyes to understanding and believing His Word, and for Him to empower you by His Spirit to obey and walk in the truth.

MEMORY VERSE

Write out this week's memory verses and one other past memory verse—Habakkuk 2:14; 1:5; 1:12; 2:4; 2:18; 3:2; 3:17–18—and crash some cymbals, if you have them.

Group Study Questions

STANDING IN UNSHAKABLE FAITH: HABAKKUK 3:16–19

- What stood out most to you from this week's lessons? How did it impact you?

- Each day this week you read Habakkuk 3 or another Scripture through a different lens. Did this give you any more insight into the passages? If so, how?

- What was one of your favorite verses from Psalm 46? Explain why the verse encouraged you.

- Did you relate to Impossible Ida, Difficult Donna, or Done Dora? Explain your answer.

- Read Revelation 21:4–7 as a group and discuss how it motivates us today.

- Discuss your thoughts on Matthew Henry's quote: "Those who, when full, enjoyed God in all, when emptied and poor, can enjoy all in God."

- Had you ever considered the concept of not asking God to *give* you strength but to ask Him to remind you He *is* your strength? If you've been praying this way, share your experience with the group.

- Which attribute of Christ most encouraged you this week?

BREAK UP INTO GROUPS OF TWO OR THREE.

Practice your memory verse with each other, share prayer requests, and then pray for each other.

> Though the fig tree should not blossom,
>   nor fruit be on the vines,
> the produce of the olive fail
>   and the fields yield no food,
> the flock be cut off from the fold
>   and there be no herd in the stalls,
> yet I will rejoice in the LORD;
>   I will take joy in the God of my salvation.
>
> **—HABAKKUK 3:17–18**

embracing

joy

A. W. Tozer

The Man of God
April 21, 1897–May 12, 1963

*Are you not from everlasting, O LORD my God, my
Holy One? We shall not die. O LORD, you have ordained
them as a judgment, and you, O Rock, have
established them for reproof.*

HABAKKUK 1:12

TODAY'S READING

Psalm 9:10; 2 Peter 1:3; Psalm 46:10

INTENT

• To know God's name means "to know him according to His
historical manifestation . . . [to call] to remembrance all that He
has done. The name is the focus in which all the rays of His actions
meet."[26]

TRUTH

In our last week together, I want us to examine how God moves us
through a life-changing progression of spiritual growth to a pinnacle
of praise. We'll also gaze into the lives of more modern-day saints who
were transformed by the God Habakkuk trusted. As He worked in His
prophet and these saints, He'll work in us and lead us to embrace joy.

Write the verses into the chart. Then pray, study the verses in context (reading enough verses before and after the passage to understand the setting, audience, and author's intent), and note truths you see.

TRUTHS ABOUT GOD	VERSE	TRUTHS ABOUT OTHERS
	Psalm 9:10	
	2 Peter 1:3	
	Psalm 46:10	

Know and Trust

As we witnessed in the life of Habakkuk, the more we know God, the more our trust in Him grows and washes away our fears and doubts—unless what we know is only enough to wet our toes.

If our knowledge of God is so thin it barely sprinkles the lies we're believing with truth, we may dampen our fears, but they'll remain to torment us.

As our trust grows through the knowledge of the Lord, our hearts find rest (2 Peter 1:3). Let's strive to know the deep things of Christ so we'll learn to trust Him deeply. He has never forsaken those who seek Him (Psalm 9:10).

Few men are as synonymous with knowing God as pastor and author A. W. Tozer. He famously said, "What comes into our minds when we think about God is the most important thing about us."[27]

We could never plumb the depths and heights of our glorious God, but like Tozer, let's try. Every second we invest in seeking to know Him better produces rich dividends of peace, power, and joy—today and forever. We can trust the Creator of time to give us the time we need to sit at His feet each day in prayer and in His Word.

Will we take the time He gives?

Pray and ask God to reveal time in your schedule to read and study His Word each day, and to climb the watchpost of your heart and spend dedicated time in prayer. Schedule it in ink and then obey.

God may call us to make sacrifices with our time to read the Bible and pray, but He'll never ask us to neglect our responsibilities. Tozer often focused so intently on God, he sometimes missed seeing those around him—like his wife and children. He wasn't perfect.

Prioritize God's Word, but go to work on time and feed the baby.

A. W. TOZER

Like a child on an Easter egg hunt, I scanned the room for hidden treasures.

A generous widow was giving away much of her husband's voluminous library. I hunted for the books that showed the most wear and tear. The ones filled with the most notes.

This is how I came to meet—and fall in love with—Aiden Wilson Tozer. The copies of his books nearly fell apart. Red ink covered almost every page. I soon understood why. Tozer's writings, more than any I'd read outside of the Bible, stirred my heart with a flame of urgency to know Yahweh—to know His name.

Tozer was born to a poor family in western Pennsylvania in 1897 and moved to Akron, Ohio, when he was fifteen. Three years later, Tozer heard a street preacher say, "If you don't know how to be saved . . . just call on God."[28]

Thus began eighteen-year-old Tozer's new life in Christ. Tozer's ministry spanned forty-four passionate years as a pastor and prolific author. His driving passion was to know God and make Him known in as radiant glory as humanly possible.

His belief fueled his urgency to write so others might also believe. During one train trip, he spent all night writing and completed one of his most beloved books, *The Pursuit of God.*

His fervor excelled such that Pastor Warren Wiersbe wrote, "To listen to Tozer preach was as safe as opening the door of a blast furnace!"[29]

Tozer didn't hold back. What one friend said of his writing could also be said of his preaching: "He left the superficial and the obvious and the trivial for others to toss around . . . [resulting] in articles and books that reached deep into the hearts of men."[30]

Wiersbe explained, "Tozer had the gift of taking a spiritual truth and holding it up to the light so that, like a diamond, every facet was seen and admired. . . . His preaching was characterized by an intensity—spiritual intensity—that penetrated one's heart and helped him to see God. . . . He so excites you about truth that you forget Tozer and reach for your Bible."[31]

Tozer wrote to send us running to know the whole Bible so we could know and trust God completely. He said, "We must not select a few favorite passages to the exclusion of others. Nothing less than a whole Bible can make a whole Christian."[32]

Tozer wasn't interested in simply accumulating academic knowledge. It's likely to produce theologians as godly as Satan. Tozer reminds us that "the devil is a better theologian than all of us put together. . . . The devil even trembles before God, but he has no part in God's kingdom."[33] Satan's view of truth and God is twisted by his pride and unbelief. Tozer said, "We can hold a correct view of truth only by daring to believe everything God has said about Himself."[34]

Tozer dared.

Will we?

The simple epitaph on Tozer's tombstone sums up the driving passion of his life:

A. W. Tozer
A Man of God

TRANSFORMATION

Jesus is infinite. "Jesus Christ is the same yesterday and today and forever" (Hebrews 13:8). "Oh, the depth of the riches and wisdom and knowledge of God! How unsearchable are his judgments and how inscrutable his ways!" (Romans 11:33). "Whoever has seen me [Jesus] has seen the Father" (John 14:9).

Tozer wrote that the words *boundless, unlimited,* and *infinite* "don't describe anything but God. . . . When you think of God or anything about God you'll have to think infinitely about God."[35]

When we think of Christ, do our thoughts rise toward infinitude, or do they sink toward someone more like us? Jesus took on flesh and dwelt among us. He hungered and thirsted like we do, but He's not like us. He was tempted in all ways and yet did not sin. His holiness can never be tainted. His power knows no end. He is God—our infinite Lord and Savior.

And we can know Him and be known by Him.

Habakkuk proved the blessing of seeking God.

Judah proved the consequences of ignoring Him.

What will our lives prove?

> With the goodness of God to desire our highest welfare, the wisdom of God to plan it, and the power of God to achieve it, what do we lack? Surely we are the most favored of all creatures.
>
> A. W. TOZER,
> *THE KNOWLEDGE OF THE HOLY*

The more we know God, the more we will trust Him.

Consider the truths in today's reading and write a response to the following question.

If I truly believe and act on what God has revealed in these passages, how will the motivations and attitudes of my heart transform and my actions be different tomorrow?

_____

_____

Pray and confess any areas of unbelief today's reading revealed. Ask God to open your eyes to understanding and believing His Word, and for Him to empower you by His Spirit to obey and walk in the truth.

MEMORY VERSE

Recite this week's memory verse aloud five times.

God, the Lord, is my strength;
    he makes my feet like the deer's;
    he makes me tread on my high places.

—HABAKKUK 3:19

Oswald Chambers

My Utmost for His Highest
July 24, 1874–November 15, 1917

I will take my stand at my watchpost and station myself
on the tower, and look out to see what he will say to me,
and what I will answer concerning my complaint.

HABAKKUK 2:1

TODAY'S READING

Psalm 143:8; Proverbs 3:5–6; Hebrews 11:17

INTENT

• *Trust* in the Bible means to have confidence, to be bold, or to be secure.[36]

TRUTH

Write the verses into the chart. Then pray, study the verses in context, and note truths you see.

TRUTHS ABOUT GOD	VERSE	TRUTHS ABOUT OTHERS
	Proverbs 3:5–6	
	Hebrews 11:17	
	Psalm 143:8	

Trust and Obey

Habakkuk trusted God, so his feet ran to obey, even though obedience required he enter the enemy's lair of captivity and remain for seventy years. The more we trust God, the more we'll obey Him, no matter the cost. He'll show us the way to go as we trust and obey, but not necessarily before we obey.

Without knowing and believing in God's unchanging character, our feet can feel mired in clay, and we are hesitant to trust or obey. But as our trust grows, our faith strengthens and shakes the clay off our feet and sends us in more eager obedience. "Can two walk together, unless they are agreed?" (Amos 3:3 NKJV).

Faith brings us to God (Ephesians 2:8–9).

Trust keeps us in step with Him and brings us joy (Colossians 1:10–11).

Habakkuk trusted God. He refused to lean on his own understanding. Instead, he climbed the watchpost of his heart to hear from Yahweh. To know the way he should go and walk in step with the One he trusted.

In what areas do you most struggle to trust God? Examine your hesitation. Are you leaning on your own understanding? Which of God's attributes will most build your trust in this area?

_____

_____

_____

_____

OSWALD CHAMBERS

Oswald Chambers responded to the gospel in his teens but experienced years of discouragement in his faith. In time, God led him to truly surrender his heart and will to Christ. To cling to God and hold all else lightly.

Immediately, Chambers's faith grew joyful legs. He traveled the world as an itinerate evangelist, passionate for the gospel that had transformed him.

On one of his trips, friends asked Chambers to keep an eye on a young lady named "Biddy" Hobbs while she traveled. He agreed and eventually promised to keep an eye on her "till death do us part." They married in 1910.

Biddy joyfully followed her husband as he followed Christ, no matter what unusual place it led them—like opening a Bible Training College in England.

He was so determined to walk in step with God that he refused to accept a wealthy patron's offer of a full endowment for the Bible college. He preferred instead to trust God daily for the funds.

"Faith is deliberate confidence in the character of God whose ways you cannot understand at the time. . . . Faith never knows where it is being led, but it loves and knows the One who is leading."[37]

A year after World War I began, God called Chambers to Cairo, Egypt, as a military missionary with the YMCA. Upon arrival, he immediately replaced the soldiers' weekly movies and concerts with Bible classes. Everyone assumed he'd fail, but instead the classes filled with several hundred soldiers, eager to hear God's Word. When he started a prayer meeting with only two men, it soon overflowed.

"Believe God is always the God you know Him to be when you are nearest to Him. Then think how unnecessary and disrespectful worry is!"[38]

While serving in Egypt, Chambers developed appendicitis. Surgeons performed an emergency appendectomy but couldn't save him.

On November 15, 1917, Oswald Chambers died at the age of forty-three. By the grace of God, he lives now in the Lord's presence, and his teachings live on in his books. Biddy had recorded her husband's messages throughout their marriage, and after she returned from Egypt with their daughter, she edited and published them.

His devotional *My Utmost for His Highest* has sold millions of copies and is translated into thirty-nine languages. His words pierce our hearts because he knew, trusted, and obeyed God with utmost devotion.

When you consider heroes of the faith like Chambers and Habakkuk, does the thought that God might ask much of you scare you? Why or why not?

_____

_____

_____

Pray through 1 Thessalonians 5:23–24 and write out verse 24.

_____

_____

What has God been calling you to do? Start a Bible college? Visit a neighbor? Forgive or ask forgiveness? What specific steps will you take today to trust and obey?

Don't compare your call to someone else's. God's spiritual gifts and callings are different for every believer—except our call to make disciples and be a faithful member of a church, serving with the gifts He's provided. This call belongs to every believer.

> Shut out every other consideration and keep yourself before God for this one thing only—My Utmost for His Highest. I am determined to be absolutely and entirely for Him and for Him alone.
>
> **OSWALD CHAMBERS,**
> _MY UTMOST FOR HIS HIGHEST_

TRANSFORMATION

Jesus is grace and truth. "And the Word became flesh and dwelt among us, and we have seen his glory, glory as of the only Son from the Father, full of grace and truth" (John 1:14).

Christ is all the grace and truth we need to trust and obey no matter what He calls us to do or endure—like Habakkuk (and Judah). The Lord's all-sufficient grace draws, empowers, and keeps us, as Chambers wrote in his journal, "Lord, keep me radiantly and joyously Thine."[39]

The more we trust God, the more we will obey Him.

Consider the truths in today's reading and write a response to the following question.

If I truly believe and act on what God has revealed in these passages, how will the motivations and attitudes of my heart transform and my actions be different tomorrow?

_____

_____

Pray and confess any areas of unbelief today's reading revealed. Ask God to open your eyes to understanding and believing His Word, and for Him to empower you by His Spirit to obey and walk in the truth.

MEMORY VERSE

Write out this week's memory verse: Habakkuk 3:19.

Jim and Elisabeth Elliot

October 8, 1927–January 8, 1956 (Jim)
December 21, 1926–June 15, 2015 (Elisabeth)

Behold, his soul is puffed up; it is not upright within him, but the righteous shall live by his faith.

HABAKKUK 2:4

TODAY'S READING

Matthew 25:21; John 14:21; 1 Corinthians 2:9

INTENT

- When Christ said in John 14:21 that He will "manifest" himself, He means He discloses His character and nature to our soul.

TRUTH

Missionary Jim Elliot once wrote to his sister Jane, "Walk as if the next step would carry you across the threshold of Heaven."[40]

His young widow, Elisabeth, later wrote, "The deepest things I have learned in my own life have come from the deepest suffering. And out of the deepest waters and the hottest fires have come the deepest things that I know about God."[41]

Write the verses into the chart. Then pray, study the verses in context, and note truths you see.

TRUTHS ABOUT GOD	VERSE	TRUTHS ABOUT OTHERS
	Matthew 25:21	
	John 14:21	
	1 Corinthians 2:9	

Obey and Experience

When we obey God, we experience aspects of His multifaceted nature. He manifests himself to us as He promised His disciples (John 14:21). We enjoy the reward of glimpses of His glory.

When we die to our pride and perceived rights and walk in obedience to His Word, His grace comforts and strengthens us. We feel His pleasure when we obey and show mercy to those who unjustly attack us.

Obedience is rewarded with spiritual treasures more wonderful than we could imagine.

Experiencing God's goodness through our obedience inspires us to more obedience, which leads to more rewards, and more obedience, and more rewards. A blessed ping-pong effect. Obedience. Reward. Obedience. Reward.

When the ping-pong effect leads to an easy life, we don't need encouragement to stay the course. But what about when the consequence of our obedience doesn't feel like a reward and leads to tears? (Habakkuk may have wondered this same question.)

JIM AND ELISABETH ELLIOT

Jim and Elisabeth Elliot obeyed God. They tasted and saw that He is good (Psalm 34:8). Their obedience gained them more than they could imagine, yet it cost them dearly. "But, as it is written, 'What no eye has seen, nor ear heard, nor the heart of man imagined, what God has prepared for those who love him'" (1 Corinthians 2:9).

Jim and Elisabeth met at Wheaton College. When they married, they expected to enjoy a long life together on the mission field. After the birth of their daughter Valerie, they settled in Ecuador with four other missionary families. They planned to befriend and share the gospel with a warrior tribe of Auca Indians, also known as the Waodani.

On January 8, 1956, Jim, Roger Youderian, Ed McCully, Pete Fleming, and their pilot, Nate Saint, landed on a sandbar with great hope. The Waodani met them with spears.

The missionaries carried guns, but they had agreed not to fire on the warriors, even if attacked. They were ready to stand before God, but the Waodani were not. And so, when the massacre began, the five men "laid down their weapons," firing only into the air.

They entrusted their lives to God—and lost them at the end of a spear.

God didn't fail the missionaries, their families, or the mission. He flung open the gates of heaven and welcomed His humble servants home. They'd fulfilled their calling.

At the same time, God's Spirit did a work of conviction in the warriors' hearts through what they saw, heard, and couldn't understand—including why the men refused to fight back.

Before his death, Nate said, "People who do not know the Lord ask why in the world we waste our lives as missionaries. They forget that they too are expending their lives. . . . [When] the bubble has burst they will have nothing of eternal significance to show for the years they have wasted."[42]

Sometime after the massacre, God sent Elisabeth and her daughter, along with Nate's sister, Rachel, to live among the warriors who'd speared the men.

Imagine how painful it must have been to obey this call. Obedience rewards.

The women got to experience the exceeding joy of leading many of the Waodani to salvation.

Mincaye—the Waodani warrior who murdered Nate—said, "Waengongi (the Creator) used his son's blood like soap. He cleaned it [Mincaye's heart], and I saw a new trail. Then I saw it's enough." Mincaye saw it was time for the brutal killings to stop. "Waengongi said, 'Come follow my trail, living well.'"[43]

Through the missionaries' obedience, God drew Mincaye to himself—and later, hundreds of other Waodani. In repentance, Mincaye vowed to care for Nate's son Steve the rest of his life. Steve's children call Mincaye "Grandfather."

Obeying God and experiencing His rewards doesn't always look like we expect. We might even say it rarely looks like we expect. God's ways are always higher than ours (Isaiah 55:8–9).

Jim Elliot once said, "He is no fool who gives what he cannot keep to gain what he cannot lose."[44]

One second, the five missionaries were standing on a sandbar facing their proud, violent attackers. No doubt the men trembled, but God gave them strength to stand in faith. The next second, they stood in the presence of the Lord.

I can imagine God saying to them, "Well done, good and faithful servant[s]. You have been faithful over a little; I will set you over much. Enter into the joy of your master" (Matthew 25:21).

Will we let sorrow crush our faith and lead us away from obedience as if God asks too much? Or instead, will we entrust our sorrow to God and let our trust in Him drive us to obedience, knowing He will empower us and never leave us?

Elisabeth described standing by their shortwave radio in the jungle of Ecuador in 1956 and hearing that her husband was missing. "The Lord brought to my mind some words from the Prophet Isaiah. 'When thou passest through the waters, I will be with thee; and through the rivers, they shall not overflow thee' (Isaiah 43:2 KJV). I prayed silently, Lord, let not the waters overflow. And He heard me and He answered me. . .

"Jim's absence thrust me, forced me, hurried me to God, my hope and my only refuge. And I learned in that experience who God is. Who He is in a way that I could never have known otherwise. And so I can say to you that suffering is an irreplaceable medium through which I learned an indispensable truth. I Am. I am the Lord. In other words, that God is God."[45]

Imagine if these men were your loved ones. Based on what you've learned in Habakkuk, list the first three truths that come to your mind that could keep you from drowning in such sorrow.

_____

_____

God takes our simple steps of obedience and does great things. What's one simple step of obedience you can take today?

_____

The more we obey God, the more we'll experience the reality of His character. Elisabeth enjoyed a full life overflowing with joy despite the sorrows she endured. But still we wonder, how many nights did she and the other widows and their children lie in their beds and echo Habakkuk's prayer, "Why, God?"

Elisabeth said, "There would be no intellectual satisfaction on this side of Heaven to that age-old question, why. Although I have not found intellectual satisfaction, I have found peace. The answer I say to you is not an explanation but a person, Jesus Christ, my Lord and my God."[46]

I think Habakkuk would sum up Elisabeth's words with God's words. "The righteous shall live by his faith" (Habakkuk 2:4).

TRANSFORMATION

Jesus is our example. "Although he [Jesus] was a son, he learned obedience through what he suffered" (Hebrews 5:8). Jesus trusted God and followed Him straight into suffering. He suffered so that we might live and reign with Him in the new heaven and new earth. When we follow Christ's example, our lives won't be easy, but they'll be glorious and lead to overwhelming and abiding joy.

The five martyred missionaries followed Christ's example and showed mercy to their attackers. They laid down their lives so the Waodoni might live and likewise know God and find salvation in Christ.

The missionaries' rewards in heaven are worth infinitely more than this world can give. The Waodoni Christians agree and lift praises of gratefulness to God.

The more we obey God, the more we will experience Him.

Consider the truths in today's reading and write a response to the following question.

If I truly believe and act on what God has revealed in these passages, how will the motivations and attitudes of my heart transform and my actions be different tomorrow?

_____

_____

Pray and confess any areas of unbelief today's reading revealed. Ask God to open your eyes to understanding and believing His Word, and for Him to empower you by His Spirit to obey and walk in the truth.

MEMORY VERSE

Write out this week's memory verse: Habakkuk 3:19.

John Newton

Amazing Grace

July 24, 1725–December 21, 1807

O LORD, I have heard the report of you, and your work,
O LORD, do I fear. In the midst of the years revive it;
in the midst of the years make it known; in wrath
remember mercy.

HABAKKUK 3:2

TODAY'S READING

1 John 4:19; John 15:9; 1 John 4:16

INTENT

• The Greek word translated *abide* in the above verses means to stay or remain, as in never leave. The word for *love* in these verses is *agape*—abiding and faithful love.

TRUTH

We love Christ because He first loved us. Period. It always starts with Him.

Write the verses into the chart. Then pray, study the verses in context, and note truths you see.

TRUTHS ABOUT GOD	VERSE	TRUTHS ABOUT OTHERS
	1 John 4:19	
	John 15:9	
	1 John 4:16	

Experience and Love

Even in Habakkuk's deepest confusion and complaints, he couldn't walk away. His knowledge of God went beyond book learning. He knew God by experience. What he knew through Scripture and experience led to some of his confusion . . . and to his devoted trust.

When God responded to Habakkuk's anguished prayers, Habakkuk experienced a fresh understanding of God's glorious nature, which deepened his love for God.

This is God's promise for all believers.

The more we trust and obey God, the more we'll experience His unchanging attributes, which ignites and deepens our love for Him. Our love will take flight and fill us with joy.

But before any of this can happen, God must give our spiritually dead souls life and open our eyes to the truth of our sin and pride. We all struggle with both. Some more desperately than others—like John Newton.

Newton called himself a wretch in his beloved hymn "Amazing Grace." He should have picked a stronger word.

JOHN NEWTON

John Newton's mother wanted him to become a faithful man of God. She devoted her life to this goal, but God interrupted her plans. Many years later Newton wrote, "[God] was pleased to reserve me for unusual proof of his patience, providence, and grace . . . by depriving me of this excellent parent when I was something under seven years old."[47]

She died.

And Newton nearly died more times than a cat. God snatched him out of death's clutches so often Newton couldn't deny God's hand.

Unusual proof of God's patience, providence, and grace.

Newton continually defied God and man. He slid into abject wretchedness and loved to drag others with him into the sewers of sin. "I often saw the necessity of religion as a means of escaping hell; but I loved sin, and was unwilling to forsake it."[48]

And still God let him live.

Unusual proof of God's patience, providence, and grace.

Newton was kidnapped and forced to serve the Royal Navy in loathsome conditions with condemned criminals. He jumped ship, was captured, and received ninety-six lashes—"a beating so brutal even one experienced member of the crew fainted."[49]

Transferred to a slave ship and then stranded on an island, he became the servant of slaves, kept alive only by the secret kindness of other slaves. He endured untold abuse, life-threatening fevers, starvation, and such desperate conditions that only God could be credited for his survival—and he hated God.

Amazing grace! How sweet the sound that saved a wretch like me!

By God's providence, a ship sent by his father miraculously found and rescued him. But on March 21, 1748, a violent storm tore at their ship and threatened to drag them to the bottom of the sea.

For the first time in many years, Newton desired God's mercy. But he thought, "What mercy can there be for me?"

He could find no rest in body or soul. Storms of every sort raged around and within him.

While he clung to life for four weeks on the sea, Newton read the Bible.

At the appointed time, Newton's battered ship miraculously limped into port with the last bite of their food boiling in a pot. God saved him both in body and soul—or at least the process had begun.

Amazing grace! How sweet the sound that saved a wretch like me!

Through His Word, God removed the scales from Newton's spiritually blind eyes bit by bit, just like He opened the eyes of the blind man and Peter in Mark 8:22–33. Christ opened their eyes bit by bit to accomplish His purposes for each stage of sight.

Newton wrote, "So wonderfully does the Lord proportion the discoveries of sin and grace; for he knows our frame, and that if he was to put forth the greatness of his power, a poor sinner would be instantly overwhelmed, and crushed as a moth."[50]

Through many dangers, toils, and snares, I have already come;
'Tis grace hath brought me safe thus far, and grace will lead me home.

Newton returned to slave trading, still blind to the egregiousness of this sin. But as he came to know Christ's love and mercy more and experience increased brokenness over sin, he saw the truth more clearly.

Newton needed only one more life-threatening fever at sea to knock off the final layer of his pride.

I once was lost, but now am found; was blind, but now I see.

Newton walked away from the slave trade industry and helped abolish it in England.

Be patient, dear Christian. God often works bit by bit. He knows how to get us—and our loved ones—from where we are to where we need to be as we experience His patience, providence, grace, mercy, and love more and more. The love Newton felt for God eclipsed all other passions he'd ever enjoyed, but he could never have known such heights of joy apart from the things he suffered.

Nobody knows the trouble I've seen.[51]

This haunting African American spiritual sings the anthem of every generation since Adam and Eve, and will until Christ returns. Nothing is new under the sun (Ecclesiastes 1:9).

Sin puts us in the position to suffer deeply—whether from our own sins or others'. But God knows all our troubles. In His wisdom, He puts us in the position to experience His joy despite suffering. But the spiritually blind unbeliever or the Christian blinded by pride cannot find this path.

Nobody knows my sorrows.[52]

Yes, Someone does. Glory hallelujah!

Christ knows deeper suffering and trouble than any of us have ever endured. And He knows your sorrows. He is with you and will lead you through.

God knew Judah's sins and the sorrows they'd suffer in Babylon, just like He knew Newton's. God was never unjust or unkind to either. Or to us.

Too often the only way we'll look up to God is from the bottom of despair.

God only takes us into suffering so He can bring us out as refined silver and shimmering gold.

If God has allowed suffering to touch you, how have you experienced His patience, providence, and grace in it? Journal your thoughts and experience.

_____

_____

_____

_____

_____

_____

_____

As you have experienced God more in your struggles, in what specific ways have you seen your love for Him grow?

_____

_____

_____

_____

_____

_____

TRANSFORMATION

Jesus is our great Savior. "For unto you is born this day in the city of David a Savior, who is Christ the Lord" (Luke 2:11). As John Newton said on his deathbed, "My memory is nearly gone; but I remember two things: That I am a great sinner, and that Christ is a great Saviour."[53]

Ironically, toward the end of Newton's life, he became physically blind. But he never lost sight of Christ's grace and mercy that drew him and saved him.

> Amazing grace, how sweet the sound.
> That saved a wretch like me.
> I once was lost but now am found,
> was blind but now I see.
>
> —John Newton, "Amazing Grace"

The more we experience God, the more we'll love Him.

Consider the truths in today's reading and write a response to the following question.

If I truly believe and act on what God has revealed in these passages, how will the motivations and attitudes of my heart transform and my actions be different tomorrow?

_____

_____

Pray and confess any areas of unbelief today's reading revealed. Ask God to open your eyes to understanding and believing His Word, and for Him to empower you by His Spirit to obey and walk in the truth.

MEMORY VERSE

Write out this week's memory verse: Habakkuk 3:19.

David and Svea Flood

God took care of me

(Svea died in 1923. Other dates are unknown.)

TODAY'S READING

For our last day together, I want us simply to soak in two glorious chapters of the Bible and one final story of God's faithfulness that leads us to embrace joy in any and every circumstance.

You'll notice there's no verse chart today. Instead, I want you to read Psalm 13 and Revelation 22 with a view toward Habakkuk and your life.

INTENT

- Habakkuk may have prayed Psalm 13 often; this short psalm mirrors the book of Habakkuk.
- Revelation 22 tells us the rest of the story—the glorious finale.

TRUTH

"These things I have spoken to you, that my joy may be in you, and that your joy may be full." John 15:11

Love and Joy

Joy isn't a destination we strive to reach. It's a fruit of the Spirit that grows sweeter the more we know, trust, obey, experience, and love Christ. This blessed pattern repeats itself endlessly and leads to joyous praise that overflows our soul.

Christ's joy is the strength we need to forget the past and smile at the future, abounding in hope . . . even if sorrow comes knocking on our door. Or in Babylon's case, knocks down our door. Abiding joy is our strength and our song as we know, trust, obey, experience, and love the Lord our God.

God Wastes Nothing

In God's merciful grace, He sent Habakkuk to tell Judah of His judgment—and the rest of their story. He comforted their souls that while they'd been unfaithful to God, God would remain faithful to them. He'd always love them, and one day He'd restore them.

Even amid God's judgment in Babylon, Judah could rejoice in the Lord and not despair the sting of regret. They couldn't rewrite their past—their evil or abandonment of God—but that's okay. He'd already written their story with His own hand, and He writes endings we could never imagine. Some of these endings include drawing us to himself in ways we would never have chosen for ourselves but which result in abiding joy.

God wastes nothing.

Sometimes He appoints furnaces of affliction. For seen and unseen purposes. And it hurts. Deeply.

Denying our grief is unhealthy.

Letting it consume us is dangerous.

In Christ, we can grieve with confident assurance that our pain has eternal and blessed purpose that leads to joy.

Sorrow doesn't have to sweep us into an abyss of bitter despair.

Our Almighty God is the context of all circumstances—both the glorious and inglorious. Even our unfixable decisions and worst rebellion.

God's holy care oversees it all.

Are you crushed by grief? Lean into Christ. His love wraps a warm blanket around us and whispers, "It's going to be okay. I'm coming like the dawn."

Has despair crushed a loved one? Tenderly share hope from Habakkuk. Let them know God hasn't forgotten them. Hope remains. (Remember this truth as you weep and pray for them.)

DAVID AND SVEA FLOOD

In 1921 David and Svea and their two-year-old son, David Jr., along with another couple, the Ericksons, trekked through the jungles of modern-day Zaire to share the gospel.[54] But no tribal chief would let them enter their village gates. With no place to live, the Floods and Ericksons built crude huts in a mountain clearing.

The local chief allowed only one young boy to visit them. He sold the missionaries chickens and eggs. Svea showered the boy with love and told him about Jesus. One day, he kneeled with Svea in repentance and surrendered to Christ.

One precious soul saved.

Over time the harsh conditions overwhelmed them. The Ericksons left their post for another, and Svea, now nine-months pregnant, suffered from malaria. The village chief relented and allowed a midwife to help her. When she finally gave birth, she could barely whisper their daughter's name. "Aina" (Ah-ee-nuh).

Seventeen days later, Svea died.

David's anguish descended into bitterness as he buried his twenty-seven-year-old wife in a grave he dug with his own hands. He'd left everything to serve God, but God had saved only one little boy and taken Svea from him. David felt abandoned, left to raise his son and sickly baby alone in that wretched jungle.

Despair and rage consumed him.

He carried baby Aina to the Ericksons and left her. He returned home to Sweden with only David Jr. and a bitter heart.

He'd abandoned his baby, his mission, and his God.

Less than a year later, natives killed the Ericksons.

Another missionary couple adopted Aina and changed her name to Aggie. When she was three years old, they returned to America.

Aggie grew up in South Dakota, attended Bible college, married Dewey Hurst, and settled in Seattle, Washington.

One day a Swedish magazine mysteriously appeared in their mailbox. Aggie flipped through its pages. A photograph of an old white cross stuck in the ground caught her eye. Two words written on the cross froze her hand in mid-flip.

Svea Flood.

Aggie rushed to a Swedish translator in a local college, where she learned her mother's story—the rest of her story.

The young boy that Svea had led to the Lord grew up and started a school. He led every child to Christ. In turn, the children led their parents to Christ. Even the chief received salvation. Six hundred souls trusted in Christ because David and Svea went to Africa, and Svea shared the gospel with one young boy.

Joy filled Aggie's heart.

Years later, Aggie and her husband traveled to Sweden where she hoped to visit her father. He'd remarried and had four more children before his second wife died. When Aggie met her siblings, they warned her that if anyone dared speak God's name in her father's presence, he exploded with rage.

Undeterred, Aggie visited him.

As she walked into his apartment, hopelessness as empty as the liquor bottles littering his bedroom filled the dreary space.

"Papa?" she said, stepping toward his bed.

David looked up. In tears, he said, "Aina, I never meant to give you away."

"It's all right, Papa," she said and embraced him. "God took care of me."

David stiffened and turned away. "God forgot all of us. Our lives have been like this because of Him."

The compassionate woman continued in a gentle voice. "Papa, I've got a little story to tell you, and it's a true one. You didn't go to Africa in vain. Mama didn't die in vain. The little boy you won to the Lord grew up to win that whole village to Jesus Christ. The one seed you planted just kept growing and growing. Today there are six hundred African people serving the Lord because you were faithful to the call of God in your life. . . . Papa, Jesus loves you. He has never hated you."

Six hundred souls serving the Lord.

Christ's love pierced David's heart. God's grace and mercy melted away his bitterness. Before the end of their visit, David bowed to the Lord he'd despised in Africa.

A few weeks later, David entered eternity.

God writes endings we could never imagine.

Sometime later, Aggie and Dewey attended an evangelism conference. The superintendent of the national church association gave a report about the spread of the gospel in Zaire. He represented over 100,000 baptized believers.

Aggie rushed to the man and asked if he'd heard of her parents, David and Svea Flood.

"Yes, madam," he said in translated French. "It was Svea Flood who led me to Jesus Christ. I was the boy who brought food to your parents before you were born. Your mother is the most famous person in our history."

Though the fig tree should not blossom,
    nor fruit be on the vines,
the produce of the olive fail
    and the fields yield no food,
the flock be cut off from the fold
    and there be no herd in the stalls,
yet I will rejoice in the LORD;
    I will take joy in the God of my salvation.
GOD, the Lord, is my strength;
    he makes my feet like the deer's;
    he makes me tread on my high places.

—HABAKKUK 3:17–19

The grace of the Lord Jesus be with all. Amen.

—REVELATION 22:21

TRANSFORMATION

Jesus is our joy. "These things I have spoken to you, that my joy may be in you, and that your joy may be full" (John 15:11).

Judah's rebellion couldn't stop or even slow God's glorious work. It did, however, rob them of blessings and eternal rewards and kept them from experiencing His abiding joy. Without true repentance and faith, rebellion would also rob them of eternal life.

But God does what we can't.

He melts hearts of stone, restores wandering hearts, and fills even the most brokenhearted with joy as we come to know, trust, obey, experience, and love Him more.

Look back at the first question in week 1, day 1, when I asked you for one word that describes the state of your heart. What word did you choose?

_____

What word best describes your heart today?

_____

What word do you think will best describe it when Christ returns?

_____

The more we know, trust, obey, experience, and love God, the more we will embrace joy.

Consider the truths in today's reading and write a response to the following question.

If I truly believe and act on what God has revealed in these passages and in the book of Habakkuk, how will the motivations and attitudes of my heart transform and my actions be different tomorrow?

_____

_____

Pray and confess any areas of unbelief today's reading revealed. Ask God to open your eyes to understanding and believing His Word, and for Him to empower you by His Spirit to obey and walk in the truth. Include your favorite memory verse in your prayer.

MEMORY VERSE

Recite all eight memory verses. How did you do?

Group Study Questions

EMBRACING JOY

• What stood out most to you from this week's lessons? How did it impact you?

• What have you found to be most helpful in ensuring faithfulness in reading your Bible and praying daily?

• When you consider the seven heroes of the faith we've looked at this week and those in the Bible, share which convicted or inspired you most. Explain your answer.

• What is your biggest hinderance to obedience? What do you think these heroes of the faith might say to encourage you?

• Share with the group your answer of the specific ways you've seen your love for God grow in your struggles as you've experienced Him more.

• What truth about Christ most encouraged you this week?

• Share the word you wrote down in week 1, day 1 that described the state of your heart and compare it with the word you chose for the state of your heart in week 8, day 5.

BREAK UP INTO GROUPS OF TWO OR THREE.

Practice your memory verse with each other, share prayer requests, and pray for each other.

> God, the Lord, is my strength;
> he makes my feet like the deer's;
> he makes me tread on my high places.
>
> —HABAKKUK 3:19

Acknowledgments

My highest thanks and praise belong to the One who is the source of all life and joy—Jesus Christ, my Lord and my God. Apart from Him, I can do nothing. Pen in hand. Eyes on God. "For from him and through him and to him are all things. To him be glory forever. Amen" (Romans 11:36).

To my whole family, you inspire me to pursue excellence . . . and joy. God has used you to help make me who I am, which gives you both part of the credit and blame. I love you so much.

Larry, since the day we said, "I do," you've made the days better, the challenges easier, and the joys more exhilarating. You've loved me to infinity, but I love you to infinity plus one. I win.

Bobby, Kaitlyn, and Samuel and Ophelia, you've covered me in love, laughter, and play breaks I desperately needed. I love you!

Brittany, you've cheered me on from across the ocean. Your love shrinks the miles and fills me with joy. I love you!

Carolyn, you designed and created the most beautiful writing studio for me. And distracted me from writing in it by being wonderful you. I love you!

Melis and Hannahbrooke, the flowers, notes, and "staying away" encouraged me and kept me focused. I'm glad you don't have to stay away anymore!

To my dear friends, I couldn't begin to list all of you who've loved, supported, and prayed for me as I've inched through the door of writing, and you inspired me with hours of exciting theological discussions. Bev, Karen L., and Grace, you literally pushed me through the writing door. Thank you. I love you all forever.

Billie Jo, you sat and talked with me for hours about Habakkuk, and now perhaps you talk with Habakkuk about me in heaven. Let's all have lunch together one day.

Traci, thanks for all the quick surprise hugs in my deadline crunch. God is good.

Mom and Dad, you were right. Studying the Old Testament is transformational. Thanks for loving God, His Word, and me . . . and paying for my first writing course.

Habakkuk Prayer Team, each week you faithfully prayed for me, and God worked miracles. Thank you. Thank you. Thank you. To God be the glory!

Lori Hatcher, my critique partner, I wouldn't want to travel the writing journey or life without you. Thank you for polishing everything I've written—twice. And even better, for praying for and with me and supplying me with milkshakes.

My dear Monketeers and Page 33 writing buddies—Lisa, Lori, Jeannie, Julie, and Elizabeth— this study and my life have been held up by your prayers, love, and critiques . . . and so much laughter.

My *Revive our Hearts* buds, Leslie, Jessica, Kim, Linda, and Renee, your passion for leading women into a deeper love for the Lord and His Word humbles, challenges, and excites me. Thanks for covering my moderator shifts so I could write and especially for covering me in prayer—Eyes on God. Pen in hand.

Pastor Jason Gillespie (Grace Bible Church), Pastor Marty Minto (Truth Tabernacle Baptist Church), and dear friend and women's Bible study leader Erin Caruso, I wouldn't have dared to attempt this project without the support of your sharp theological eyes and insight. I praise God for men and women who are as committed to sound teaching and faithfulness to God's Word as you.

Grace Bible Church (Lexington, SC), I never dreamed when we women studied Habakkuk together that it would end up as a book. Thank you for your abounding love for God, His Word, my family, and me.

New Testament Baptist Church Women's Bible study group, thank you for helping me write this study and realize that an eight-week study is better than four.

Lexington Word Weavers and Word Weavers International, you all drive me to excellence and made this journey an exciting adventure. Thank you!

My editors Rachel Kirsch, Linnae Conkel, and Sarah De Mey. You are all truly a gift from God. The study is stronger because of each of you.

Our Daily Bread Ministries, thank you for giving me this amazing opportunity to bring the life-changing truths of Habakkuk into the hearts and homes of many. I'm honored to serve the Lord with you. I thank you and your staff for your commitment to doing all we humanly can to provide a transformational study that's faithful to the Lord.

To every reader, I'm overwhelmed with gratitude that you would join me in this journey through Habakkuk. Writing this study has been one of the greatest experiences of my life. I've prayed continuously that the truths God proclaimed through our beloved prophet won't simply inform you but transform you.

It's all about Him!

Jean

Notes

1. O. Palmer Robertson, "Habakkuk #01: The Dialogue of Protest," sermon, February 1, 2004, https://www.sermonaudio.com/sermoninfo .asp?SID=2180472415.

2. "Strong's H4853—*maśśā*'," BlueLetterBible.org, accessed August 15, 2022, https://www.blueletterbible.org/lexicon/h4853/kjv/wlc/0-1.

3. "Strong's G281—*amēn*," BlueLetterBible.org, accessed August 15, 2022, https://www.blueletterbible.org/lexicon/g281/esv/mgnt/0-1.

4. "281. amen," BibleHub.com, accessed August 15, 2022, https://biblehub.com /greek/281.htm.

5. *NKJV Cultural Backgrounds Study Bible* (Grand Rapids: Zondervan, 2017), 1594.

6. Ibid. pg. 1195.

7. Ibid. pg. 1594–1595.

8. Ibid. pg. 1595.

9. "Strong's H6918—*qādôš*," BlueLetterBible.org, accessed August 15, 2022, https://www.blueletterbible.org/lexicon/h6918/kjv/wlc/0-1.

10. O. Palmer Robertson, *The Books of Nahum, Habakkuk, and Zephaniah* (Grand Rapids, MI: Eerdmans, 1990), 151.

11. Elisabeth Elliot, *Suffering Is Never for Nothing* (Nashville, TN: B&H, 2019), 100–101.

12. Steven Lawson, "Fortress for Truth: Martin Luther," Ligonier Ministries, October 5, 2018, https://www.ligonier.org/blog/fortress-truth-martin-luther.

13. O. Palmer Robertson, *The Books of Nahum, Habakkuk, and Zephaniah*, The New International Commentary on the Old Testament (Grand Rapids, MI: Eerdmans, 1990), 174.

14. Robert Jamieson, A. R. Fausset, and David Brown, *A Commentary, Critical and Explanatory, on the Old and New Testaments*, vol. 1 (Hartford, CT: S. S. Scranton, 1871), 704. Also available at "Habakkuk 2:16," BibleHub.com, accessed August 25, 2022, https://biblehub.com/commentaries/jfb/habakkuk/2.htm.

15. G. K. Beale, "Does God Ever Give Christians Over to Their Idols?" *Theology for Life 7*, no. 1 (Spring 2020): 32, https://servantsofgrace.org/wp-content /uploads/2020/04/Idolatry-The-Secret-Sin-of-the-Heart.pdf.

16. John Calvin, *Institutes of the Christian Religion*, trans. Henry Beveridge (Peabody, MA: Hendrickson, 2008), 55.

17. C. H. Spurgeon, *The Power of Prayer in a Believer's Life* (Lynnwood, WA: Emerald Books, 1993), 94.

18. Martin Luther, quoted in J. Oswald Sanders, *Spiritual Leadership: Principles of Excellence for Every Believer* (Chicago: Moody, 2007), 100.

19. Elisabeth Elliot, *God's Guidance: A Slow and Certain Light* (Grand Rapids, MI: Fleming H. Revell, 1992), 18.

20. "Strong's H433—'elôha," BlueLetterBible.org, accessed August 17, 2022, https://www.blueletterbible.org/lexicon/h433/kjv/wlc/0-1.

21. "What Does *Selah* Mean in the Bible?" GotQuestions.org, accessed August 24, 2022, https://www.gotquestions.org/selah.html.

22. Carl Friedrich Keil and Franz Delitzsch, *Commentary on Habakkuk* (n.p.: Titus Books, 2014), 1053. Also available at "Habakkuk 3:12," BibleHub.com, accessed August 25, 2022, https://biblehub.com/commentaries/kad/habakkuk/3.htm.

23. https://uhg.readthedocs.io/en/latest/verb_cohortative.html.

24. Carl Friedrich Keil and Franz Delitzsch, *Biblical Commentary on the Old Testament: The Twelve Minor Prophets*, vol. II (Edinburgh: T&T Clark, 1868), 115. Also available at "Habakkuk 3:18," BibleHub.com, accessed August 25, 2022, https://biblehub.com/commentaries/kad/habakkuk/3.htm.

25. Dr. and Mrs. Howard Taylor, *Hudson Taylor's Spiritual Secret* (Chicago: Moody, 2009), 165.

26. Ernst Hengstenberg, "Commentary on Psalms 9," Hengstenberg on John, Revelation, Ecclesiastes, Ezekiel, and Psalms, accessed August 18, 2022, https://www.studylight.org/commentaries/eng/heg/psalms-9.html.

27. A. W. Tozer, *The Knowledge of the Holy* (New York: Harper and Row, 1961), 9.

28. "A. W. Tozer—Short Biography," SermonIndex.net, accessed May 21, 2022, www.sermonindex.net/modules/articles/index.php?aid=150&view=article.

29. Warren W. Wiersbe, *50 People Every Christian Should Know* (Grand Rapids, MI: Baker Books, 2009), 352.

30. A. W. Tozer, *The Mystery of the Holy Spirit*, ed. James L. Snyder (2007; repr., Newberry, FL: Bridge-Logos, 2019), 4–5.

31. Warren W. Wiersbe, introduction to *A Treasury of A. W. Tozer: A Collection of Tozer Favorites*, by A. W. Tozer (Harrisburg, PA: Christian Publications, 1980), 9.

32. A. W. Tozer, *Of God and Men* (Chicago: Moody, 2015), 77.

33. A. W. Tozer, *The Dangers of a Shallow Faith* (Bloomington, MN: Bethany House, 2012), 23.

34. A. W. Tozer, *The Knowledge of the Holy* (San Francisco: Harper & Row, 1961), 86.

35. A. W. Tozer, *The Attributes of God*, vol. 1 (Chicago: WingSpread, 2007), 4.

36. "Strong's H982—*bātah*," Blue Letter Bible, accessed May 21, 2022, www
.blueletterbible.org/lexicon/h982/kjv/wlc/0-1.

37. Oswald Chambers, *The Quotable Oswald Chambers*, comp. and ed. David
McCasland (Grand Rapids, MI: Discovery House, 2008), 94.

38. Oswald Chambers, "January 2," in *My Utmost for His Highest* (Grand Rapids,
MI: Discovery House, 1992).

39. Wiersbe, *50 People Every Christian Should Know*, 323.

40. Elisabeth Elliott, *Shadow of the Almighty* (San Francisco: Harper & Row, 1956),
53.

41. Elisabeth Elliott, *Suffering Is Never for Nothing* (Nashville: B&H, 2019), 9.

42. Russell T. Hitt, *Jungle Pilot: The Gripping Story of the Life and Witness of Nate
Saint, Martyred Missionary to Ecuador* (Grand Rapids, MI: Discovery House, 1997),
142.

43. Richard N. Ostling, "Famed Missionary Martyrdom Ultimately Saved the
Assailants' Tribe," *Arizona Daily Sun*, January 20, 2006, https://azdailysun
.com/famed-missionary-martyrdom-ultimately-saved-the-assailants-tribe
/article_1d608770-8544-59df-a691–6424e79fd03a.html.

44. Elliot, *Shadow of the Almighty*, 15.

45. Elliot, *Suffering Is Never for Nothing*, 1, 15.

46. Elliot, *Suffering Is Never for Nothing*, 12.

47. John Newton, *The Life of John Newton* (New York: American Tract Society,
1854), 9.

48. Newton, *Life of John Newton*, 11.

49. Stephen Davey, *Legacies of Light: Modern Heroes of the Faith* (Cary, NC: Charity
House, 2019), 121.

50. John Newton, "Salvation at Sea," in *Early Evangelicalism*, ed. Jonathan M.
Yeager (New York: Oxford University Press, 2013), 232.

51. "Nobody Knows the Trouble I See," Hymnary.org, accessed August 19, 2022,
https://hymnary.org/text/sometimes_im_up_sometimes_im_down_oh_yes.

52. "Nobody Knows the Trouble I See."

53. William Jay, *The Autobiography of the Rev. William Jay*, vol. 1, ed. George
Redford and John Angell James (New York: Robert Carter & Brothers, 1855), 316.

54. All quotes came from Davey, *Legacies of Light*, 3–13.

Spread the Word
by Doing One Thing.

- Give a copy of this book as a gift.

- Share the QR code link via your social media.

- Write a review of this book on your blog, favorite bookseller's website, or at ODB.org/store.

- Recommend this book to your church, small group, or book club.

Connect with us. [f] [o] [y]

Our Daily Bread Publishing
PO Box 3566, Grand Rapids, MI 49501, USA
Email: books@odb.org